Syncl

Voyage

by
Susan Heather Ross

This book is dedicated to the wonderful people who have
shared experiences with me and the teachers that I
have learned from throughout my life.
Without each of you, this book could not have been written.
Thank you...

Figure 1

www.owlsage.com

"Aho Mitakuye Oyasin" – Lakota prayer

All my relations

We are all one...

Acknowledgements

My loving family has given me the tools, confidence, and support to live a meaningful life and has never judged my choices. They are generous, caring, and have always had my back.

My partner Nick is an amazing man whom I love deeply. We have enjoyed many years together and know that we can count on one another in life. I am lucky and grateful to have him by my side. He is my best friend and my rock.

All of my wonderful friends, many of whom have shared some synchronistic experiences with me, are an invaluable part of my life. It would be difficult to thank each of them individually, so I am thanking them collectively.

The acquaintances who briefly encountered synchronicity with me are also a vital part of my stories, which would not have taken place without them, wherever they may be today.

My friend Louann is both intuitive and wise. She has been supportive and nurturing throughout the journey of me writing my book and has provided insightful feedback along the way.

The teachers and sages whom I have learned from in-person, as well as through books and other sources, have been a tremendous inspiration to me on my life path. They have also guided my writing in many ways.

Lastly, I am grateful for the naysayers who have challenged me with the belief that humans are just biological entities in a meaningless universe. Perhaps my book will inspire them to consider the possibility that there is a miraculous and meaningful order within the cosmos.

"The lips of wisdom are closed, except to the ears of understanding"- The Kybalion

Table of Contents

The Prologue

"Synchronicity is an ever-present reality for those who have eyes to see"[1]- Carl Gustav Jung

The story you are about to read unfolds as a series of unusual and unexplainable coincidences that have happened throughout my life. The events seem to flow spontaneously in waves of messages and signs linked together in patterns that have no logical explanations. Synchronicity is the term used to describe these patterns of intertwined coincidences by many people who have experienced the phenomenon. When it occurs, it is an exhilarating feeling of a connection to something beyond ordinary, everyday existence. It feels like a shift in reality where you are in the midst of something miraculous that defies the laws of probability on an unprecedented scale. You question the statistical likelihood of such a fully integrated pattern of events taking place that seems like an impossible set of circumstances. It feels as though both internal and external forces are mysteriously guiding you.

There are people all over the world who have had synchronistic experiences. A variety of books have been written on the subject by authors such as Deepak Chopra, who explores the connection between quantum physics and synchronicity. *The Celestine Prophecy*, by James Redfield, was one of my first introductions to the concept over thirty years ago. I was intrigued by the story and the idea that coincidences have important messages to convey. I didn't realize back then that I was about to embark on a journey with synchronicity, and that it would become such a an extraordinary part of my life.[2]

Carl Gustav Jung, a Swiss psychiatrist, and psychoanalyst who founded *Analytical Psychology* is said to have coined the term synchronicity. He defines it as being an "acausal connecting principle," believing that coincidences had an underlying meaning for an individual or group. He documented one of his sessions with a patient who refused to see the deeper meaning in her life. She was in the middle of describing a dream she had in which she was given a golden scarab beetle when suddenly, Jung heard a light tapping at a window. Upon opening it, a golden beetle flew into the room. Jung felt that the scarab beetle was a classical symbol of rebirth and transformation, as seen in some ancient belief systems such as Egyptology. Realizing the significance, he showed the beetle to his patient after catching it in his hand, which enabled her to begin viewing her life from a new perspective, and she made much progress in her therapy sessions.[3]

Carl Jung explored the concept of what he termed the "collective unconscious," in which humans seemed to be connected within a part of the brain sharing universal thoughts and experiences, which developed into archetypes and mythologies in cultures around the world.[4]

A quote attributed to Jung states, "In all chaos, there is a cosmos, in all disorder a secret order" exemplifying the idea that although events may seem random, there is an underlying order existing within that connects them. Manifesting synchronicity requires an awareness of messages conveyed through a variety of "concurrences," which are repeating occurrences such as the appearance of relevant and meaningful symbols. Jung stated, "What I found were coincidences which were connected so meaningfully that their chance *concurrence* would represent a degree of improbability that would have to be expressed by an astronomical figure."[5]

Symbols contain a vast array of powerful ideas and concepts and can play an important role in synchronistic experiences. They have been used throughout history as a means of communication from the simple to the very complex. They can hold great mysteries just waiting to be revealed to an individual ready to receive the wisdom. The spiral is an ancient symbol representing the cycles of life, death, and rebirth, the structure and growth of many life forms in nature, and spiral galaxies in the universe. The *Aum* symbol represents the first primordial sound, and the *Yin Yang* symbolizes the polarity principle and balance in the cosmos. I will reveal the essential meaning of symbols like these in greater detail, as they are an integral part of the events that have taken place in my life.

Synchronicity is the key to how our known universe developed. The remarkable set of coincidences, such as the temperature and speed of expansion, leading to the creation of stars, planets, and galaxies, is mind-boggling. The force of gravity and the speed of light are perfectly

—

calibrated and harmonized as well. The position of the sun, moon, and earth had to be situated exactly where they are for life to exist on earth, as well as the size of each and the relative distance between them. If any of the conditions were remotely changed, space would have been devoid of stars, planets, and life forms.

Furthermore, the rising and setting of the sun and moon held special significance in both the survival and spiritual beliefs of humankind. Many cultures have left behind clues as to how they devised a way to calculate these cycles and transformations that had a synchronistic way of operating.

Albert Einstein was quoted as saying, "He (God) does not play dice with the universe" and was also believed to have said, "There are only two ways to live your life. One is as though nothing is a miracle. The other, as though everything is a miracle."[6]

As you read and view the images, I encourage you to keep an open mind and put aside overly rational thought or stringent religious beliefs. What I am about to share with you has happened to me. Some of you may have experienced synchronicity and will read my stories with the feeling that you are not alone. Others will be skeptical, which is to be expected. I was skeptical once too.

Life is cyclical, so I will describe some peak experiences and reflect on how they have unfolded and circled back through my life. I have been sharing my stories with people around the world, and they often react with the comment, "You should write a book," to which I have always responded, "Maybe one day..."

Part One

Transformation

Embrace the Unknown

Evolve and Thrive

Chapter 1
The Hero's Journey

"We must be willing to give up the life we planned so as to have the life that is waiting for us."[7]- Joseph Campbell

The Power of Myth

Joseph Campbell (1904-1987) was a prolific writer and teacher of comparative mythology, customs, religion, and spirituality, whose words have been surfacing throughout my life just at the right time for me to hear them. He had the gift of presenting a total worldview of cultural stories that were threaded together like a finely woven tapestry with a colorful pattern. His wisdom has forever impacted many people around the world, and I am one of them.

The first time that I encountered his brilliance was in a literature course in college at Hofstra University in New York, where I was earning a teaching degree. The professor showed the class a video of Campbell in an interview with Bill Moyers that was known as *The Power of Myth* series. He spoke to me, and I listened. His riveting discourse about the meaning of life and his words, "follow your bliss," struck a chord within me. I wanted to travel, see the world, and hear the stories of the people everywhere. I also longed to create my own stories.

Joseph Campbell recently appeared in my life once again on Netflix. *The Power of Myth,* which I had not seen since that class, happened to be featured as a movie suggestion, and I watched the series from an entirely new perspective. It impacted me today just as it had in the past but in a much broader and more meaningful way.[8]

The Hero and the Flag

The following synchronicity took place soon after I began writing the first part of this chapter. I was planning to write about Joseph Campbell's explanation of a recurrent theme in mythology called *The Hero's Journey* and was taking time to collect my thoughts. I am a high school ceramics and design crafts teacher and have been teaching for over twenty-five years. There is a student enrolled in my class who has been struggling with many things. I see the light in him, but he is lost in the darkness. On his first day, he opted not to stand for the pledge of

—

allegiance during the morning announcements. There has been much controversy surrounding standing for the pledge in recent months, so I asked him why he chose to sit. The student responded that our government is corrupt and that he doesn't do things just because he is told to do them. As I stood with my hand over my heart, I explained that I do so to honor the brave hero soldiers who have sacrificed their lives so that we have the freedom to choose to sit or stand. He seemed to have a change of heart soon after.

I was looking through some of the assignments for his other classes and noticed that his English teacher had given him one on *The Hero's Journey*... I was amazed that I had planned to write about it, as well as my discussion with the student about hero soldiers. The assignment was based on Joseph Campbell's book, *The Hero with a Thousand Faces,* where he describes the different stages of this journey as a theme of courage, growth, transformation, and wisdom that is prevalent in most myths around the world.

Campbell identifies a variety of archetypes, such as the hero, mentor, ally, shadow, etc. who appear in mythology as well as in our own lives. He felt that they were the embodiment of a set of characteristics that most people can identify with at one time or another. There are archetypes in every culture throughout history, some well-known and others more obscure.[9]

Stages of the Hero's Journey
According to Campbell's *Mononmyth,* the hero experiences a call to face the abyss of the unknown world to gain something of physical, emotional, mental, and spiritual value. At first, the hero denies the call to adventure until it inevitably becomes a quest or journey that he/she feels compelled to embark on, and a decision is made to leave the ordinary world and dive into the abyss.

During the separation stage or jumping-off point, the hero realizes that fear is a major inhibitor and that in order to have a transformative experience, he/she must cross the threshold into the unknown. This idea is reflected in Campbell's quote, "It is by going down into the abyss that we recover the treasures of life."[10]- Joseph Campbell

There is a point where the hero faces fears, challenges, obstacles, or enemies with some guidance from the archetypes of the separation stage who are the threshold guardians. They can appear as mentors, teachers, role models, and spirit guides who lead, aid, and protect the hero on his/her quest.

The Hero's Journey is a death to one's old self and atonement with the new self. It is a rebirth into a life of acceptance, meaning, and wisdom, which is like a snake shedding its' skin to be born anew. The higher perspective and awareness that develops once the hero undergoes the final stages of transformation is considered the boon or reward. The most important part of the journey is for the hero to integrate the lessons from the experiences into everyday life after returning from the quest and share the boon of wisdom with others.[11]

The brilliant George Lucas, who created the *Star Wars Trilogy*, was a friend of Joseph Campbell, and they often spent time together at his home called *Skywalker Ranch*. It had been said that Joseph Campbell's work inspired George Lucas to create *Star Wars* and that it embodies *The Hero's Journey*.[12]

The theme of *The Hero's Journey* is also relevant in the lives of ordinary people who have triumphed by facing fears, challenges, and doubts through a metamorphosis process, much like a butterfly. The cocoon represents the inward journey and the call to transform into something new. The caterpillar doesn't hesitate or fear the painful process of becoming a butterfly; it just dives in and creates the conditions from cocoon to chrysalis to butterfly. It is a metaphor for accepting life's changes and spreading one's wings open to the possibilities that lie ahead, no matter how intimidating and daunting that threshold can be. We are all on our own *Hero's Journey*.

I have truly embraced the wisdom of Joseph Campbell's words. They have been a great source of inspiration for me to venture into the abyss with fearless confidence. As a result, I have had many incredible experiences that have changed my life and exciting stories to share.

"What the caterpillar calls the end of the world, the master calls a butterfly."[13]- Richard Bach

Chapter 2
Animal Spirit Guides

Message, Journey and Life Totems

Storytelling is one of the most compelling forms of communication and has been a part of the human experience since the dawn of civilization. Animals and mythological creatures are featured in myths, legends, and fairytales as symbols to express something that may have been witnessed by an individual or group, or a belief held by the people of that time. Many profound ideas and events have been recorded through orally shared stories and written traditions. They often depict sacred animals who possess desirable characteristics such as strength, resilience, wisdom, and compassion.

In many native cultures, animals have spiritual counterparts known as totems that act as guides from the unseen world. It is believed that they have aided humans throughout history, as is evidenced by the many expressions of them in art, literature, and picture writing such as petroglyphs and hieroglyphs.

There are four main categories of totems; message, journey, life, and shadow. I will address the shadow totem in a later chapter. They are often referred to as medicine due to the healing effects of one's interaction with them, and I have personally had some compelling experiences with totems in my life.

Butterfly Message

Message totems appear sporadically, and a person may encounter one or several of them multiple times in his/her lifetime. They arrive at the moment we are either contemplating an important decision, about to go through a transformation, or when we simply need to pay attention to something. They can also be a great source of comfort as a sign from a loved one who has passed. The key is to be open and aware enough to recognize and appreciate the significance of the brief but special visit from a message totem.

I had an experience with butterfly medicine many years ago when I made a decision that would change the trajectory of my life. I had gone to a psychic whom a good friend urged me to visit due to her incredible

—

reading. I was very skeptical of people claiming to have psychic abilities but decided to visit with her out of sheer curiosity. She was an elderly woman whose home contained piles of books lining all the hallways and open areas. It was strangely inviting as I was seated at a small table that had a tarot deck in the center. She didn't ask me any questions as she was shuffling the deck and arranging the cards on the table that manifested to the surface.

She began interpreting the messages and relayed to me that I was going to meet a man with a one-year-old daughter and that my life would turn in another direction once I met him. She also said that I would move across the country to Nevada and teach art in three different elementary schools. At the time, I was living in New York and happily teaching high school ceramics and design crafts. I had also just received tenure that year, which was an important milestone in my career. I grew up on Long Island, where most of my family still currently resides, and couldn't fathom leaving them, my friends, my job, and my comfortable life.

As it turned out, the psychic was right, and I met my ex-fiancé a few years later, who had a one-year-old daughter at the time. We had an immediate connection, and soon after, we began traveling the world together and having great adventures. Although we were living in New York, he started doing business with the arcade industry in Las Vegas, Nevada, and I recalled what the psychic had predicted, as it was always in the back of my mind. When his business began thriving, he asked me if I would consider the possibility of moving there in the future, so I told him about the psychic and that I would be willing to check it out. A few weeks after our conversation, we headed to Vegas.

I fell in love with the quiet beauty of the desert landscape, the warm, dry climate, and fun nightlife. I was in my early thirties, adventurous, and enjoying life to the fullest, so it was an exciting proposition to move across the country while also being quite daunting at the same time. I recalled the prediction that I would teach elementary art in three schools and felt that if I applied for a job and was offered a position like that, it would be the ultimate sign that I should move. I decided to interview at a public school district with my credentials as an Art Specialist K-12 (all grade levels) and was informed that I had to accept the first offer given to me or be denied employment in the district for up to a year. A few weeks after submitting the application, I received a call from a principal offering me a position in elementary art in three different schools... I almost dropped the phone after hearing the offer and then excitedly accepted it. I moved across the country soon after being hired and taught elementary art for the first year and middle school art for two years after that. I missed teaching high school, so I decided to interview for a position at a brand new school, got the job, and was thrilled to be teaching on the secondary level once again.

My ex and I lived together for over ten years and enjoyed many great events, concerts, restaurants, bars, and an assortment of interesting places together. We traveled to various countries, stayed at amazing hotels, visited monuments, castles, and museums, ate fantastic food, and drank the best wines. We met people from all walks of life and had wild adventures with great stories to tell after our experiences. I will always cherish those memories. They shaped who I am today, and I am grateful for the life we shared. Unfortunately, our relationship had become strained for a variety of reasons, and we slowly began drifting apart as a result. It was during that time that I discovered the numerous benefits of yoga. I loved the way that the *asanas* (poses) made me feel strong, balanced, flexible, and confident. They also made me feel relaxed, happy, and peaceful. I soon developed a rigorous yoga practice and began delving much deeper into spirituality and yoga philosophy, which changed the way I thought and felt.

One day while practicing at a local studio, I was overcome with a sense of gratitude for how yoga was affecting me in such positive ways that I decided I wanted to become an instructor. I signed up for a yoga teacher training in Santa Barbara, California for the summer and was looking forward to celebrating my fortieth birthday in May before my training. I noticed that butterflies kept appearing everywhere in very unusual ways, which was often a sign that a change was about to take place in my life. I had a gut instinct that was so strong that I decided to get a butterfly tattoo to represent the change that I sensed I was about to go through. I designed it to be a part of an earlier tattoo on my right ankle that I got after an incredible trip to Iceland years before that reads *Carpe Diem*, which is Latin for "seize the day." It was very fitting to incorporate my hand-drawn image into the tattoo as a butterfly is a perfect symbol for *Carpe Diem*, due to its' brief lifespan.

A couple of months later I discovered that my instinct and intuition were correct. My ex and I mutually decided to part ways a few days before my birthday, realizing that we weren't moving in a compatible direction in life. We had a very amicable, though difficult and painful break-up. He was my best friend, and my heart ached so badly after he moved out of the home we shared for many years. I am very thankful for the wonderful experiences we shared and also for his generosity. At the time of our breakup, however, I was glad that I was leaving for my yoga teacher training a month later, where I knew I would begin healing. I wrote a poem the day before I left, and bought a beautiful pink robe with a crystal butterfly on the back to take with me as a reminder of my intention to spread my wings and fly.

Transformation
The caterpillar makes its way
Crawling through the night and day
Until the time a change must come
To hide away like the setting sun
A shelter is made
A change takes hold
Until the caterpillar
Breaks through the mold
The transformation is complete
The butterfly has shed her feet
To spread her wings
And fly free
Enjoying the liberation
Just to be… - Susan Heather Ross

I traveled to the *White Lotus Foundation* retreat in Santa Barbara and arrived there early, so I decided to go into town with a few of the women who got there at the same time as well. We visited a thrift shop where I happened to find a shirt with a flaming heart on it and bought it to symbolize how I was feeling. I was focused on healing my heart while fanning the flame that was ignited within it as well.

Upon returning to the retreat to check-in and settle into our chosen accommodations, I couldn't believe my eyes… There was a sculpture of a flaming heart right beneath my sleeping quarters, and I knew that it was a sign that I was on the right path.

My experience at the retreat was life-changing, as I had a feeling it would be. I met great people, ate delicious and healthy food, practiced yoga, laughed, and began the healing process. When I returned home after my training, I was renewed with a sense of purpose and enthusiasm that had the momentum of a gazelle. My training inspired me to delve more deeply into yoga philosophy, and I couldn't wait to teach my first class. I was so excited to be able to share yoga with others so that they could experience the incredible benefits and blissful effects as well.

I started a yoga club at my high school once the summer was over, and the new year began, which I have had every year since then. I have also practiced yoga with students who were emotionally disturbed, autistic, learning disabled, and handicapped, which has been both humbling and gratifying.

Yoga has enriched my life in very profound ways and has taught me that change is necessary for growth. The symbolism of the butterfly totem continues to remind me to let go of what was to make room for what will be...

Butterflies and the Spirit World

A message totem may appear at a key moment when an individual is thinking of a deceased loved one as a messenger from the spirit world. Several years ago, I met a gentleman through a friend who told me about his synchronistic encounter with a butterfly totem that was very inspiring. He was on a business trip out of town when he received a call from his wife that his beloved golden retriever had fallen ill. He immediately booked a flight home but unfortunately didn't make it in time. Upon returning home and learning about the passing of his best friend, he was wracked with unimaginable grief.

He fell into a deep depression and could barely function while he struggled to go through the motions of his daily life. Day after day, he found himself sitting under a large tree in his yard where he used to spend time with his buddy in a deep well of sadness. His grief was compounded by the fact that he didn't make it home in time to say goodbye. Being a dog lover myself, I could feel his pain and had tears in my eyes as he told his story.

One day, while sitting under the special tree, a beautiful, brilliant, orange butterfly landed right next to him. He said that it seemed to be looking at him while it opened and closed its wings in a mesmerizing pattern of movement. After what felt to him like a timeless moment, it flew away, and he decided to research the symbolism by looking up the words *orange butterfly symbol*. To his amazement, an image of a golden retriever with a butterfly on its' snout matching the one that appeared to him popped up on his screen with the caption, *Golden Butterfly*... He believed that the butterfly's appearance was a message from his dog and felt an incredible sense of peace and solace from the experience. His story is not uncommon, as many people have reported signs from loved ones through the appearance of butterflies.

My mother had a similar interaction with a butterfly totem while she was visiting my great grandmother's grave and silently asked for a sign that her spirit was out there somewhere. At that precise moment, a butterfly landed on her nose and stayed for a few seconds. My mother felt it was a message from her and was very comforted by the sudden appearance of the totem. She had another butterfly encounter during her best friend's funeral when one landed on the casket as she was asking for a sign from her friend, and she was reassured once again.

There is a collective, spiritual, and synchronistic event that occurs every year. It is the migration of millions of Monarch butterflies from various parts of the world to Mexico during *Dia de Los Muertos (Day of the Dead)*, which is a festival honoring the deceased friends and relatives of the people of Mexico. They magically appear at the same time as the festival year after year, and it is believed that the butterflies represent the souls of their ancestors. It is a very sacred tradition and celebration, which genuinely reflects humankind's connection to the spirit world through animal totems.

Wolf Journey

A journey totem is an animal or insect that will appear when specific guidance or protection is needed and will often enter one's life for an extended period to aid in a more in-depth experience of self-reflection. The journey totem that I have encountered throughout my life has been the wolf. Ever since I was a young child, I have felt a connection to wolves. I can recall when I was in the third grade that I made a clay wolf sculpture, and my art teacher remarked that I was very talented with clay. Interestingly, I became a ceramics high school teacher many years later.

The wolf totem has been surfacing at various times in my life to teach me many things about courage, instinct, strength, and freedom. I have always felt very protected by the energy and power of wolf medicine and own a variety of sculptures, pictures, shirts, and decorative items of wolves. I have a poster of a black wolf with a caption below it that says, *Risk: Trust Your Instincts,* which has been hanging on my wall for many years as a visual reminder to trust my inner voice.

The Pendant & the Train

When I was a young art teacher, I met a student named Jada who was enrolled in a painting class in my department at the high school where I was teaching at the time in New York. I happened to be on hall duty when she approached me on her way to class, and I noticed her wolf pendant. When I complimented her on it, she informed me that she had made it, which sparked a conversation about jewelry making and our mutual fascination with wolves. My students were creating beaded jewelry at the time, so I invited her to my classroom to see what they were making. She stopped by a few days later and I allowed her to make some pieces, which she enjoyed very much.

I made arrangements with Jada's painting teacher for her to join my class after she completed her assignments, and we found that we had much in common, as we were both very inspired to travel the world and learn about cultures from other lands. She graduated high school that year with plans to attend college to earn a degree in the arts, and we kept in touch through written letters as she embarked on her journey through life.

Jada and I lost contact for a while, as she was living abroad, and I had moved to Las Vegas but ran into each other when I was visiting my family in New York. I was taking a train to NYC to see a concert and was thinking about the fact that she and I hadn't spoken in over a year. A few minutes later, I looked up at the door between train cars, and she just happened to be walking through it at that very moment...

After we got over the initial surprise, she informed me of her possible plans to study Flamenco dancing at a university in New Mexico but was still on the fence about what she wanted to pursue next. She had just returned to the USA from the Australian outback, where she lived among the aborigines and learned how to dance with fire. Before that, she lived in Costa Rica and was a member of a performing trapeze group. She said that she wanted to continue following her passion, so I invited her to visit me to check out some opportunities that might interest her, which proved to be a pivotal turning point in her life.

She took me up on my offer, visited for a couple of weeks, and then moved to Las Vegas a few months later, where she thrived for many years as an artist, performer, yoga instructor, studio owner, author, wife, and mother.

Jada and her family relocated to Canada and currently live in a home they built off the grid in the wilderness that runs almost entirely on solar energy. The story of how they braved the harsh winters in a tiny RV on their property until they were able to build a home is very inspirational. They are true pioneers and have created a beautiful space called *Barefoot Sanctua*ry, where they host spiritual retreats for people from around the world.[14]

Before she left the USA, Jada gave me the wolf pendant she made that resulted in our friendship, and I was very touched by the gesture.

The Invitation

I was taking a break from writing this chapter and decided to check the time on my phone when I saw that I had missed a call from Jada. I was amazed by the fact that I had just written about her, so I called her back right away and excitedly told her that I was writing a book and that she was a part of my story. I mentioned the synchronicity of her calling me as I was writing about her in relation to the wolf totem. She then informed me that she had recently gotten a new puppy that was part wolf named Timber... I also had just adopted a puppy and named him Marley. He came to me in a synchronistic way through the wolf totem, which will be revealed later.

The most intriguing part of our communication was when she told me that she had planned to host a women's retreat in Canada. She had just created a flyer with the information and was about to send an invitation via text to a list of women she thought might be interested in attending. It just happened to be one of the reasons that she called me, so I asked her to send it to me, and I was astounded when I read it.

The theme of the retreat was related to the book *Women Who Run with the Wolves* by Clarissa Pinkola Estés, which is about female archetypes in mythology throughout history and how they are symbolically relevant to the lives of all women... The author is a Jungian analyst (Carl Jung), and the overall theme of the book is the female (*heroine*) *Hero's Journey* (Joseph Campbell).[15]

Jada's Wolf Pendant

Wild in the Wilderness
Yoga Retreat 🕯 🍃 🔥
May 16-19

Join Jada and guest teachers for a sweet journey into primal nature, fire flow yoga, primitive skills and wolf wisdom.

Suggested reading for this journey is the magical and profound book, Women who Run with the Wolves by Clarissa Pinkola Estes, as there will be highlights and teachings related to this realm of story.

At the end of our remarkable conversation, I thanked Jada for the invitation but unfortunately wasn't able to attend. After we hung up, I thought about what had just transpired between us and the fact that she and I have had several other synchronistic events take place throughout our many years of friendship.

It felt like a confirmation that I was on the right track in the direction I was heading with my writing. I have recently had some experiences with the wolf totem, which actually inspired me to write this book. I struggled for a while, trying to figure out how I wanted the timeline to flow and was guided to *trust my instincts*.

Anubis, Thoth, and Cerberus

Life totems are partners and guardians in our earthly existence. They enter our lives in many different ways through visions, dreams, out-of-body experiences, channeling, and in-person. They guide, protect, and challenge us to learn, grow, and become wise. In the Native American culture, young boys are initiated into manhood by going on a *Vision Quest* for three days alone in the wilderness to find their life totems. There are many similar initiation rituals connecting humans with their animal spirit guides in various cultures around the world.

I was introduced to my life totem in a way that can only be described as otherworldly. It all began many years ago when I met a fellow teacher who taught science and often took her students on field trips as part of her curriculum. We didn't know each other very well at the time, but she asked me to be a chaperone on a weekend student field trip. I was honored that she thought of me, and I happily accepted the request.

After a fun and informative day, she told me that the reason she asked me to be a chaperone was that she felt that I was a very positive person, which sparked a conversation about energy and the universe. We spoke about the connection between science and spirituality when she revealed to me that she was able to channel information from a group of higher-level beings in the spirit world. I was skeptical at first, as I usually am about people who claim to be clairvoyant, but also intrigued because she was a well-respected and intelligent teacher.

She began telling me a story about her son and two of his friends using a *Ouija Board* to contact ancient Egypt one afternoon in a desert cave, which was said to have a powerful vortex of energy. As they started moving the cursor over the board, they each became quite disoriented and then quickly decided to put the board away soon after feeling the strange effect it was having on them.

Later that evening, one of the boys had a frightening dream that he was being led down a long, dark, stone passageway towards a large gate by *Anubis*, an Egyptian deity with a jackal's head and a human body. He is usually pictured in hieroglyphics holding an ancient cross with an oval at the top called an *ankh* in his hand, which is a very potent Egyptian symbol of the eternal life force. He was believed to preside over the embalming ceremonies and was considered a guardian of the underworld. He is often depicted with a *Scale of Justice* that has a *Feather of Truth* on one side, and the heart of a deceased person on the other. The scale was used in a ceremony known as the *Weighing of the Heart* in the *Hall of Maat*. If the person's heart was lighter than the feather, the soul could pass on to the afterlife, if it was heavier than the feather, the soul was devoured by a demon goddess called *Ammit* and delivered to the hellish underworld known as *Duat* to pay a karmic debt. Anubis was believed to be the benevolent protector of lost souls in the afterlife, also known as *The Field of Reeds*.

Another figure that the young man reported seeing in his dream was *Thoth*, the Egyptian deity of wisdom, writing, and magic, who was inscribing something on the wall as he was being led towards the ominous gate looming in the distance. Thoth is often depicted with an Ibis bird's head and a human body and is believed to have incarnated on earth several times throughout history in various places such as Atlantis, Egypt, and Greece. He is considered to be the author of an ancient manuscript known as *The Emerald Tablets*, which contains the profound wisdom of universal laws and principles. It has been said that he is the recorder, scribe, and messenger of the *Akashic Record*, which is described as a living account of every possible past, present, and future event and thing existing in the universe, including all thoughts, deeds, and actions. He is often pictured in Egyptology writing on a scroll manuscript to symbolize his power as the record keeper of the cosmos. He also had the role of recording the karmic fate of the deceased during the *Weighing of the Heart* ceremony.

I could feel a tingling in my spine while she continued the story. As Anubis and the boy approached the enormous double gate, there was a decrepit old man pointing his finger and fiercely scolding at him in an unfamiliar language. Suddenly, a giant three-headed dog known as *Cerberus,* who was thought to be the guardian of the underworld in ancient Greek mythology, appeared behind the old man and lunged ferociously while the massive gate slowly creaked open...

The frightened boy was jolted awake and sat up, trembling in his bed. I could only imagine how traumatized he must have been as I thought about the symbolism of his dream. I wondered if he had done something in his life that warranted a visit from these entities and if he had possibly opened some kind of portal with the *Ouija Board*. When I asked her if anything happened to the boy after the dream, she was not sure, as her son had lost touch with him. I was left with some mixed feelings about what she had told me and was not sure what to make of her story, but it most definitely piqued my interest.

I have always embraced the idea of karmic justice and was fascinated by Anubis and Thoth after hearing of them. I didn't know at the time that the information she revealed to me would spark a chain of events that would greatly affect my life.

Thoth   Anubis   Ankh   Cerberus

The Council of Elders

The following Monday morning after the field trip, I was teaching an art lesson on Surrealism and looking forward to seeing the unique compositions that my students would create with the concept. As the first class of the day began the project, a student approached my desk and asked if I could help him with an image he wished to include in his drawing, which just happened to be of Cerberus, the three-headed dog.

At first, I thought it was just a strange coincidence and proceeded to open my cabinet, where I kept a variety of books on symbolism and mythology. My attention was immediately drawn to a book called *Animal Spirits*, so I took it off the shelf, opened it to a random page, and was stunned when I gazed at the images before me. On the bottom of the left page was an image of Anubis and on the top of the right page, an image of Cerberus… I was completely freaked out as I had never experienced synchronicity on that level before, but I didn't want to alarm my student, so I just played it off like a simple coincidence. He remarked that he had dreamt about Cerberus chasing after him, which is why he wanted to include it in his drawing. I thought quietly to myself that there must be some reason why these entities are appearing through dreams to the boys and wondered why I was now a part of it by opening the book to the page.

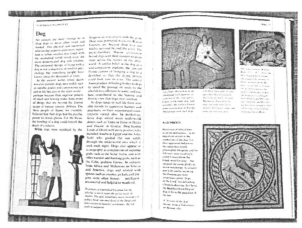

Figure 2

I spent the rest of the day contemplating the meaning of the bizarre occurrence. I met with my friend after work to speak with her about it, and she didn't seem very surprised. She said that she knew that I would be receiving a sign, which, of course, made me want to know more. She asked me if I would be okay with her contacting her spirit guides for some insight to which I agreed, so she sat down in front of her computer and began channeling through automatic writing. It seemed as though she was in a trance while she typed very rapidly, not even taking a break to collect her thoughts. After about five minutes of continuous typing, she printed what had come through, and we began reading. It was written in English but a strange, unfamiliar style and was like a letter of introduction from the spirit world starting with the greeting, "Salutations." They introduced themselves to me as *The Council of Elders* and proceeded to tell me about the nature of reality and the structure of the universe. They spoke of different dimensions and realms of existence and the multitude of life forms out there. They informed me that I had a connection to them through symbols and signs and that I would be receiving messages as long as I was *vigilant and aware*. The synchronicity that took place that morning was a sign for me to pay attention to the symbols, as they would be instrumental in my life. They said that they could not reveal the true meaning of my experience that morning and that it was up to me to discover that for myself. My friend was told that they wanted her to channel from my home as they had some vital information to share with me there. I was so excited and curious that I invited her over the following weekend.

The Owl & Gabriel

As my friend entered my home, she immediately sensed a presence and described it as wolf/dog energy. That didn't surprise me in the least considering my connection to both. She sat down on the couch with her laptop and began typing rapidly and nonstop, just like the first time. She relayed to me that *The Council* told her that I should go to a particular mirror that was hanging on the wall around the corner and look at my reflection because I would be given a sign. The frame of the mirror was Native American themed and adorned with leather, fur, feathers, a painted symbol of the four directions, and a spiral. Without hesitation, I walked up to it, and I stared deeply into my reflection, feeling like a warrior. At first, I didn't notice anything significant, so I kept looking deeper into my eyes when suddenly, my face seemed to transform into an owl for a split second. As I explained the strange vision to my friend, she then instructed me to sit down in my living room because they said that I was going to receive another sign. My attention was then drawn to a shelf as a beam of sunlight shone on a *Kachina* doll that was given to me by the mother of my ex-fiancé. It belonged to her mother, who had recently passed, and she said that she felt compelled to give it to me for some reason.

Kachina dolls are sacred effigies that are an essential part of many Native American tribes. They are imbued with spiritual qualities and are often depicted with a human body and an animal head, similar to the deities in Egyptian hieroglyphics and carvings. They represent the spiritual forces of the universe through nature in the form of humans, animals, plants, and minerals and act as intermediaries between humans and the spirit world.

I lifted my Kachina from the shelf and realized, to my amazement, that it was an owl… I looked underneath the bottom and saw that it was signed *Great Horned Owl Kachina* by the artist. As I stared in disbelief at the effigy, my friend proceeded to tell me some incredible life-altering information that she was receiving for me from The Council.

Figure 3

I was told that my spirit guide and protector was called *Gabriel,* and the owl was the totem that would appear as a sign when he/she was present. It was then revealed to me that there was a moment when he/she crossed the veil and spoke to me. I knew right away what The Council was referring to and felt as though I was in a whirlwind of intense energy.

Crossing the Veil

I recalled the time many years ago when I heard a voice speak within me while driving back to college in the Hamptons in New York late one evening. I was alone in my car on a very desolate road, which was lined with thick, large trees on either side. It was a pretty creepy scene like something from the set of a scary movie. I was driving along in silence as my cassette tape had just ended when I heard a low voice say in a straightforward command, "slow down, put your high beams on, look up ahead at the bushes." It was very unnerving, as I had never experienced anything like that before and was usually skeptical of people who claimed to be told things by the spirit world.

I felt urged to listen and slowed my vehicle to about 15mph, turned my high beams on, and looked towards the right side of the road expecting a deer to run out as there were many in the area. I noticed some rustling movement in the trees up ahead when all of a sudden, a deranged-looking man wearing tattered army clothing darted out and started running towards me. He dove headfirst in front of my car as I quickly swerved to the left and avoided hitting him by some miracle. My instinct told me not to stop as this man was obviously crazy, so I kept driving in a state of shock. I could see him in my rear-view mirror, just standing in the middle of the road while watching me drive away. It was most definitely like a scene from a horror flick where the victim escapes unharmed but totally traumatized. Cell phones hadn't been invented yet, so I couldn't call anyone and had a long drive ahead to reach my destination. I was frightened and shaking the entire time.

It was very late when I finally arrived at my school, and I called the police from a payphone on campus. I told them what happened and the area that the man was closest to at the time of the incident. They thanked me for the tip and assured me that they would investigate the situation. Everyone was asleep, so I had to sit with what had occurred by myself until the next morning. When I told my friends the story, they were as mystified as I was. I had a difficult time processing the creepy encounter and could not stop thinking about the voice I heard inside of me.

About a week after the incident, I happened to see a copy of the newspaper, and the crazy man's face was on the front page... The caption read something like "Wanted Man Found Dead in his Home," and as I proceeded to read it, I was shocked. The man was on the FBI's most-wanted list for several years for a series of heinous crimes, including rape and murder. He must have known that the FBI was close to catching him and attempted to commit suicide by diving in front of my car. When that plan failed, and the FBI started closing in on him, he blew himself up with a hand grenade in the basement of his home rather than being captured.

I was utterly dumbfounded after reading the article and left with many questions but no answers. I have always wondered about that night and who warned me of the possible danger. When I briefly described the experience to my friend, she told me that The Council said that I was protected and spared by Gabriel crossing the veil at that moment. They informed her that I was a "Symbologist," and that I would write a book someday about the significance of important symbols and the meaning they would have throughout my life. At the time, I couldn't imagine what adventures the future had in store for me and that I would write a book about them.

The Sage Feather

The experience of being shown my life totem has always made me feel that my home is a protected and sacred space. A few years later, I decided to have a tile floor installed one spring, and I hired a tile expert who happened to be Native American. He commented on some of the cultural artifacts displayed around my home, remarking that they were powerful and authentic and asked me if I knew my life totem, so I began telling him my story.

After describing my encounter with The Council and being shown the owl through the mirror and the Kachina doll, he asked me to see the mirror. I had brought him over to where it was hanging, and he requested that I remove it from the wall so he could see the other side of it. I had never thought of looking at the back and was curious as to why he asked to see it, so I took it off the wall and turned it over.

To my absolute astonishment, the writing on the back read *Owl Feather Studio, Sedona Arizona...* I had no idea that the connection was behind the mirror the whole time until my chance conversation with the man. I then showed him the Kachina doll, and he confirmed that I was indeed introduced to my life totem. I researched the mirror after that and found that the last name of the artist who created it was Gabriel... When I realized the magnitude of my discovery, it felt like yet another clue to some spiritual mystery.

Several years after that incredible synchronistic confirmation of my life totem, I had yet another one in Sedona, where I had purchased the mirror. The captivating landscape is like a jewel in the middle of the desert with its striking red rock formations that resemble giant chiseled sculptures. I have had many mystical experiences while visiting there over the years. It is believed that there are vortexes of energy in the area, which I have felt, and the quaint town of Sedona has many crystal shops, art galleries, vortex tours, and psychics.

During one of my many trips there, I went shopping at a store called
Crystal Magic and bought some sage and a beautiful abalone sage
bowl.[16] Sage is an herb that has been used to clear discordant energy by
many cultures around the world for thousands of years. It has both
medicinal and spiritual properties, and the word sage means wisdom,
which the owl represents.

I had completed my purchase and was leaving the store when my
attention was drawn to a cabinet that had something jutting out from
behind it, so I decided to check it out because I felt a strange pull
towards it. I removed it from the wall and realized that it was a
smudge fan made of feathers that is used to fan the smoke of burning
sage during a space clearing ceremony. I felt that it was a sign that I
should buy it because I had just bought the sage and a bowl.

As I was holding it and admiring the beautiful craftsmanship, I turned
it around and was astounded when I saw that it was signed with the
name Gabriel... I was totally caught off guard but then quickly realized
the significance of the message and went back to the register to buy it.

At the time, I was experiencing some disharmonious energy that
needed to be eradicated, which is why I had bought the sage. When I
returned home after my trip, I conducted a sage ceremony with the
four cardinal directions using my new fan. I focused on the elements of
earth, air, fire, and water to purify the space as the sage smoke
dissipated throughout, which seemed to help clear the heavy energy.

I have always felt that I was guided to find the smudge fan to use as a
spiritual tool to remove negativity throughout my life. It is presently
draped over the owl totem mirror on the wall in my home as a
reminder of the mysterious connection between them.

| Back of Mirror | Sage Feather | Handle (Gabriel) |

The Bad Owl Cafe

As I have been writing each chapter, I have also been gathering the photos that I planned to include in the stories. I located the book *Animal Spirits*, which is the one that I had opened eighteen years ago so that I could take a photo of the images of Anubis and Cerberus. I decided to open it randomly again before turning to the intended pages, and there was a picture of a soaring owl. It was an awesome image, so I took a photo of it and posted it on social media, which sparked a dialogue with a childhood friend who said she was planning to get a wise old owl tattoo to represent her mother who passed. There was also a comment on the post from a former student of mine named Erica. She mentioned that she was recently visited in person by both a Great Horned Owl and a Barn Owl on two separate occasions and that the messages from both were life-changing. I was curious about her experiences after communicating back and forth a few times and suggested that we meet for coffee at a café called *The Bad Owl*, as that would be a very fitting place under the circumstances. She agreed, so we made plans to get together.

Erica Nicole
I had never seen an owl in real life growing up here. Then August of last year a huge great horned owl flew over me and landed on a tree at the park. Then in December, I saw my second owl this time a barn owl, in the Home Depot parking lot on the ground. We had a silent exchange for a solid minute until he flew into a tree. These owls were huge messengers for me and helped guide me to the choices I landed to now. So powerful!!!!!! I'm going to get a tattoo of one as well.

43m   Like   Reply   Message   ◎¹

Figure 4

Erica and I met at *The Bad Owl* cafe a week later as planned, and we sat down at a table with our lattes. I mentioned that my story was about synchronicity and that I was first introduced to the concept by the book *The Celestine Prophecy* when she politely interjected and said, "I know about that book because you gave it to me to read in high school." She reminded me that I had let her read it outside my classroom on the adjacent patio during class when she seemed troubled and that it had a major impact on her life.

At that point, she began telling me her story of the visitation from a Great Horned Owl while she was hiking in the desert. She was thinking about a particularly challenging situation in her personal life when the owl appeared and watched her from a tree. It was an intense moment for her, as she felt that she was being given a sign that it was time to make some crucial decisions. The visitation gave her the courage and wisdom to make the changes, which had a positive outcome. A few months later, she spotted another owl that was just sitting in the middle of a parking lot and staring at her. I told her that I felt that the first owl inspired her to be wise and confident and that the second owl was confirmation that she made the right choice.

As we continued our conversation, she reached into her purse and retrieved a small gemstone owl charm that she gave to me, and I was very touched. We recalled the time that we saw each other about ten years ago when she happened to attend a tarot card reading at my home. The tarot deck that was presented was titled *Ancient Animal Wisdom* and was co-created by Jada, and a woman named Stacey, who contacted Jada to collaborate with her to design the cards.

I was not aware at the time that Erica and Jada were friends through Stacey, and they both just happened to have been my former students from two opposite coasts. It was also synchronistic that the cards contained inspirational messages of animal wisdom, and Erica and I were discussing the subject of animal totems years later because of the owl picture that I had posted.[17]

As we were marveling at the synchronicities that were occurring, I noticed her purse had a golden key on the zipper. I then pointed out to her that part of the décor on the wall was also a golden key.

It is truly amazing what you can see when your eyes and mind are open. After a couple of hours of enlightening conversation and great coffee, we hugged goodbye with plans to see each other again soon.

Figure 5

Erica posted this heartfelt message on social media after our meeting...

 **Inspired To Shine**
January 26, 2019 · ⊙

Teachers can have such an impact. When I was in high school I switched schools a total of 4 times before graduating my junior year, it wasn't a fun time for me. In 9th grade, if my one close friend didn't show up for school I would sit alone or hide in a hall. The one thing I looked forward to was my art and ceramics classes. Ms. Ross was the coolest teacher, I loved her because she had traveled a lot and would always teach me about the world, I never told her but she knew how lost I felt and how much I questioned my existence without me having to say anything. She would let me sit outside in the sun and introduced me to the book The Celestine Prophecy that year. I didn't go back to that school the next year, but I never forgot her, or the books she introduced me to. 10 years later I got invited to a women's gathering at someone's personal home, it was to my surprise and amazement that the home was in fact Ms. Ross's. This was only the beginning of many synchronistic stories that would unfold in my adult life, giving me constant confirmation that I was headed in the best possible direction, to just keep going. Today, 17 years after meeting her, she treated me to coffee and we talked about the book she's writing and again she taught me things, like the meaning of Aho Mitakuye Oyasin, meaning: all my relations. All things are connected, so all things have impact on each other so directly, we just can't always see it so soon. I live my life as homage to all the people like my art teacher who have impacted my life in such significant ways. I will continue to pay it forward as I am so grateful. May you never doubt your existence or impact.🙏🦉
.
.
.
.

#teachersrock #lasvegasschools #synchronicities #life #meaning

Chapter 3
The Envelope & The Buddha

Mysterious Images

The following morning after my conversation with Erica, my wonderful partner in life, Nick, informed me that he just watched a movie where a Great Horned Owl was featured. He knew that it was significant in my story, so he recorded it to able to show it to me. He paused the scene of an owl perched on the branch of a tree, (which also looked like a soaring owl) so that I could take a picture. I used my flash in the photo that caused a very unusual bright orb to appear perfectly placed over the owl's head, that wasn't the typical looking effect of a flash. I left for work soon after with the feeling that more signs might be coming my way, so I was *vigilant and aware.*

I arrived in my classroom and noticed a large envelope sticking out of my bookshelf. Feeling that there may be a significant find, I opened it and discovered two images that were relevant to my story.

Blue Medicine Buddha & The Mandala

The first image I retrieved from the envelope was a card with a photo of a *Blue Medicine Buddha* painting on the front. It was connected to an experience that I planned to write about, which also took place in Sedona during a family trip with my mother and two sisters. We stayed at a beautiful resort called *Enchantment* and visited many of the shops and galleries in town. One of the galleries, *The Goldstein Gallery*, featured Tibetan Monks creating a sacred, colorful sand *mandala.*[18]

A *Mandala* is an ancient Indian Sanskrit term and concept which translates to the word circle in English. They are prevalent throughout nature in forms such as the head of a sunflower, snowflakes, tree rings, the human eye, blood cells, DNA, etc. as well as being the shape of planets, moons, and stars in the cosmos. Mandalas are also works of art and have been used symbolically for centuries in art, architecture, and sacred structures around the world.

Carl Jung felt that the mandala represented growth, transformation, unity, and wholeness and that it could be used as a symbol to express both the inner world of the individual and the outer world of nature and the universe. In a period of self-reflection, he stated, "I saw that everything, all paths I had been following, all steps I had taken, were leading back to a single point - namely, to the mid-point. It became increasingly plain to me that the mandala is the center. It is the exponent of all paths. It is the path to the center, to individuation."[19]

The Tibetan monks design sand mandalas using a variety of sacred symbols, images, and deities to represent spiritual concepts that promote compassion and world peace. They have been creating them for centuries by using a special tool to carefully place the tiny grains of colored sand within a circular, precisely drawn outline of a symbol that represents different aspects of the divine universe called a *Yantra*.

Each grain of sand is blessed and infused with positive intentions, and mandalas are created to embody a *Cosmogram* or blueprint of the cosmos and the fleeting moments in life. Tibetan Buddhism teaches the importance of detachment by accepting things as they are and embracing change with the wisdom that it is necessary for growth.

After the entire mandala is finished, the monks sweep the sand into the center to represent impermanence and the idea that the soul is eternal, as energy can never be created nor destroyed; it simply changes form. They place the blessed sand into a golden vessel and ceremoniously release it into a moving body of water. It is believed that the water will evaporate with the positive imprint of the infused sand and eventually rain down on the human race, thusly raising the level of consciousness on the planet. It is a beautiful tradition and symbolic gesture of compassion for all sentient beings.

I had never seen the creation of a mandala live before, and the gallery presented a fantastic opportunity to experience it in an intimate setting. The timing was perfect to view the ritual as I was planning on teaching an art lesson on mandalas when I returned home from my trip. The students create their mandalas based on chosen symbols representing their lives, dreams, and beliefs. It is incredibly therapeutic for them, and each one is special and unique.

Figure 6   *Figure 7*

As the monks were lovingly creating the mandala, my family was admiring the superb artistry throughout the gallery. There was an eclectic variety of paintings, sculptures, and jewelry displayed in the space, and we felt like kids in a candy shop. An artist whose work was featured there had painted magnificent pointillist (tiny dots of color) renditions of a variety of Buddhas. My sister Kimberly was immediately drawn to a *Blue Medicine Buddha* painting, which symbolized healing, good health, and longevity. As a doctor of holistic medicine, she often recites a prayer, which invokes the healing power of that particular Buddha. She was enthralled with the painting, but it was a bit too large for her meditation space, so she asked the manager if there was a smaller version and was told that there wasn't one available at the moment. Just then, the artist of the painting walked into the gallery, introduced herself as Shey, and began speaking with us about her work and inspiration for creating the series. She said that she had spent many years as a Tibetan nun living at a monastery and described her technique as using the dots of color, similar to creating a sand mandala, by infusing each dot with positive energy as she paints. It was indeed an honor speaking with such a wise and talented woman as she shared about her background and artwork. My sister asked her if it was possible to commission her to paint the *Blue Medicine Buddha* in a

smaller size, and she responded that she had already done so, and it was in the back room. The manager retrieved the painting, after apologizing for the misunderstanding, which turned out to be the perfect size for the area that my sister wanted to display it. Shey informed us that it was special because she had written a Tibetan prayer on the back of it, which she usually doesn't do. Incredibly, the inscription was the exact *Blue Medicine Buddha* prayer my sister regularly recites during meditation as a mantra for healing;
Om Be-kan-dze Be-kan-dze Ma-ha Be-kan-dze Ra-dza Sa-mung-ga-te So-ha...
"To the Bhagawan with equal compassion for all, Whose name when just heard dispels lower realms' suffering, Dispeller of disease and the three poisons prostrate to Medicine Buddha Lapis Light."

Needless to say, my sister purchased the painting, and we went back to our resort to relax for the evening, feeling inspired by the experience.

Figure 8

The following morning my sister Laura had informed us that she discovered on social media that a young boy she knew had gone missing in the town where she resides in New Jersey. She was upset and concerned, as we all were, so we decided to sit inside the crystal meditation room at our resort and focus our intentions and prayers on the boy being found. The three of us each recited our special mantras (prayers) while the sun shone through the glass dome window above us on the large crystals in the center, creating a cascade of brilliant patterns of light throughout the space. Soon after we finished our mantra recitations, Laura got an alert on her phone that the boy was found unharmed and was back with his family. I learned never to underestimate the power of prayer that day.

Hyde & Seek

The second image that I discovered in the envelope was a rough sketch I had done many years ago of a female form with long hair, a bent knee, and her arms reaching upwards towards a man who is hiding his face from her. I later created a sculptural, ceramic vase of the sketch and hid the word *Hyde* (a play on words) along the man's spine and *seek* along the woman's spine as they were engaged in a game of *Hide and Seek*.

Many years after creating both the drawing and vase, my grandmother passed away, and I was in her home after her funeral. I noticed a beautiful art deco ceramic sculpture of a female form that I realized upon further inspection was strikingly similar to the one that I had made... The long hair, arms reaching upward, and the shape and positioning of the feet and hands were almost identical, with a couple of minor variations, to my vase. I had never seen the sculpture before, and my mother confirmed that it was relatively new, and she wasn't sure about its' origin.

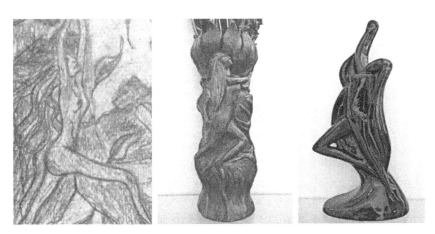

I brought it back home with me, and it has been displayed next to my vase ever since. I was considering including the story in the book a few days before finding the sketch. Perhaps it was a message from my grandmother, "Seek and ye shall find."- Mathew (verse 7:7)

Words of Wisdom

I entered my classroom again the following morning, and my attention was drawn to a small scrapbook on the same bookshelf, which I made after a trip to Bali, Indonesia. During my visit there, I stayed at a lovely resort, and it was delightful to find cards with quotes that were written on them from wise people such as Anne Frank and the Dali Lama placed on my bed as part of the turndown service in the evenings. I saved them with the idea that I might use them for a project in the future. When I returned home from my trip, I created a collage scrapbook using some of the quote cards and a variety of images. I titled it *Words of Wisdom* and placed a paper cutout image of an owl on the front cover.

I removed it from the shelf and opened it to the first page, which had images of both the Great Horned Owl and Buddha arranged above one of the cards with a quote from the Dali Lama below that said, "Train yourself to take in what is going well and view the rest with wise detachment."- The Dali Lama

The fact that I had just written about Buddhism, detachment, and the Great Horned Owl was yet another sign for me. The synchronicity that seems to happen while I am writing each chapter has enabled me to reflect on my experiences more in-depth, which has been invaluable.

The concept of detachment is described as the liberation from earthly desires and cravings. As humans, many of us tend to feel that we will attain happiness once we satisfy whatever it is that we crave, such as food, jewelry, cars, sex, drugs, money, and love... The result is that

many people often live in a state of lack with an overwhelming feeling of needing something or someone to be happy. It is considered to be the root of suffering and one of the main reasons why there is much strife in the world today. The key to living happily and peacefully is to detach from our desires by living fully in the moment. Buddhism teaches that through meditation and training the mind, one can be freed from the bondage of perpetual longing. It requires patience and awareness, which is known as *mindfulness.*

Buddhist teachings include the concepts of reincarnation, karma, and the *Wheel of Dharma*. It is believed that each soul reincarnates as many different life forms. There is a karmic bond to past lives that must be mitigated in this lifetime, or one will continue to incarnate over and over again to get it right and move to a higher plane of existence. Each person's karma is said to be connected to the *Wheel of Dharma*, which is rooted in ancient wisdom and considered to be the moral code and cosmic order of the universe. Once a person becomes fully awakened, he/she is said to have achieved *Buddhahood*, also referred to as enlightenment or *Nirvana*. The Buddha, who attained this enlightened state, paved the way for others to do so through his teachings known as Buddhism.

Siddhartha Gautama
Buddhism began with the life of The Buddha, who was born a prince named Siddhartha Gautama in the kingdom of Nepal during the 6th century B.C. His mother had a dream while pregnant that she gave birth to a white elephant through the side of her torso, which was said to be a very auspicious sign that she would bear a son who would either be a great military leader or a spiritual teacher. The premonition was a problem for the king, who desired to expand his kingdom and continue his legacy through his son. Sadly, Siddhartha's mother died a week after his birth, and he was raised in a lavish lifestyle befitting a future king and military leader. His father took great pains to shelter his son from the outside world, as well as his mother's death, so he grew up not knowing the truth of human existence and suffering. He had never been exposed to the reality outside of the magnificent palace as the king forbade him to leave.

One day, Siddhartha had a chance meeting with a visitor who told him about the beauty of springtime. He wished to see the colorful flowers and green grass described by the visitor and implored his father to allow him to venture outside to view the spectacle. To satisfy his son's curiosity, the king carefully orchestrated a springtime procession outside of the palace walls where he eliminated all signs of suffering, old age, poverty, illness, and death from view. However, there was a glitch in the scheme when Siddhartha saw an elderly man walking down an alleyway. His father had sheltered him from the truth that people age by only allowing young people to live in his kingdom and disguising his age as well. Upon seeing the old man, Siddhartha asked his aide for an explanation to which he replied that all people age and that he too would become old one day. The startling revelation prompted Siddhartha to leave the procession and investigate further where he encountered the poor and sick as well as a corpse. His entire world was turned upside down, and he could no longer live the idyllic, sheltered existence he had only known before the truth was revealed to him.

He had a wife and newborn son whom he named *Rahula*, which translates to fetter or anchor, indicating that he felt his son would keep him tied to his life at the palace if he didn't make a decision quickly to leave. Although he loved his wife and son dearly, he knew he must dive into the abyss to discover the true nature of reality and how to liberate oneself from suffering. He quietly left the palace in the middle of the night without saying goodbye to his loved ones for fear that he would not depart and wandered off into the wilderness.

He initially found a *guru* (teacher) who was unable to help him on his quest, so he joined a group of *ascetics* (religious zealots). They had been attempting to liberate themselves from their bodies through self-mutilation, deprivation, starvation, and being naked in hostile conditions. Siddhartha quickly became the most revered ascetic due to his extreme attempts to detach from his physical form by standing on one leg for days at a time, hanging upside down from a tree, and starving himself to the point of being close to death's door. However, he was no closer to enlightenment through the brutal practices than he was before he embarked on his *Hero's Journey*.

Feeling lost, dejected, and slowly dying of starvation, he encountered a young woman who handed him a bowl of rice, saying simply, "Eat this." Buddha decided at that moment to abandon his extreme measures of self-mutilation as he gratefully accepted the bowl of rice and instantly felt a wave of relief and happiness. It is said that soon after eating the rice, he overheard a music teacher instructing his student, "If you tighten the string too much, it will break, not enough, and it will be too slack," which caused him to have a major epiphany... He realized that the key to being peaceful and happy was to live in balance in all aspects of one's daily life and to detach from the binding chains of longing, suffering, and fear in the material world.

The revelation was so profound that he felt compelled to sit under a Bodhi tree and not move until he reached enlightenment, referred to as *Nirvana*. He sat for seven days, during which time the demonic *Mara* (Lord of desire) appeared trying to tempt him with earthly delights to lure him away from reaching Nirvana. He resisted and grounded himself by touching his hand to the earth while having a vision of the entire cosmic wheel of life, death, and rebirth. It was at that moment that he became The Buddha which means, "awakened one."

The Buddha called the discovery that led to his awakening, *The Middle Way*, or *Eightfold Path*. It is said that he delivered a simple but powerful message during one of his early sermons as he held a flower in his palms, saying nothing the entire time. Only a few people understood the meaning of the message at first, but then many became his disciples, including his wife and son, as they realized the life-changing concepts in his teachings. He traveled throughout India sharing his wisdom with millions of people for over fifty years during his lifetime.

The Buddha taught his followers that both happiness and fulfillment come from gratitude, compassion, and living in the present. He died at eighty years of age from food poisoning but consoled his grief-stricken disciples while on his deathbed by assuring them that he, and they, are eternal. His teachings continue to inspire many millions of aspirants to awaken around the world.

As a side note, it just happened to be the anniversary of the Buddha's transition from this incarnation to the next called *Nirvana Day* while I was writing the story of his life...

Buddha Quotes

"My friends, it is through the establishment of the lovely clarity of mindfulness that you can let go of grasping after past and future, overcome attachment and grief, abandon all clinging and anxiety, and awaken an unshakable freedom of heart, here and now."

"Work out your own salvation. Do not depend on others."

"If you find no one to support you on your spiritual path, walk alone."

"Peace comes from within. Do not seek it without."

"One who acts on truth is happy in this world and beyond."

"The mind is everything; what you think you become."

"Nothing can harm you as much as your own thoughts unguarded."

"There is no fear for one whose mind is not filled with desires."

"Even death is not to be feared by one who has lived wisely."

- The Buddha

Part Two

Nomadic Journey

Travel the Path of the Soul

You Will Find Yourself There

Chapter 4
Epiphanies in Europe

Zen Viking

I go through periods in my life where I embrace the concepts of detachment and mindfulness, while other times I buy things I don't need and tend to form attachments to objects and outcomes. For some reason, I also feel drawn to learning about ancient barbaric cultures, and I like to watch movies and television shows about the history of warlike people such as the Romans, the Mongolians, and the Vikings. I took a course in college about the barbarians throughout history and was both horrified and fascinated by them.

I believe in the possibility of reincarnation, and I have felt throughout my life that I may have been a Viking, although I have no rational explanation for the feeling. I have a warrior-like mentality when it comes to defending myself and others, as well as being fearless in my pursuits, adventures, and travels. I also enjoy earthly, material pleasures, and tend to desire and covet beautiful things.

The Viking way of life was the epitome of what Buddhism describes as the root of all suffering, which is desire and attachment. They had an insatiable appetite for power and were rife with greed, lust, and violence, so it is a bit conflicting that I would feel a connection to them yet also be drawn to Buddhist teachings as well. A disturbing and brutal historical fact is that they often robbed and pillaged the Buddhist monasteries and slaughtered all the monks. I could never imagine participating in a Viking raid and killing innocent people but feel that if my territory had been under attack, I would've defended my village to the death if necessary for survival. Perhaps that was my role among my people, and I did not participate in the raids. I may have initially enjoyed the artifacts, which were brutally taken from others, and then at some point, had a shift in my consciousness, which changed my perspective.

It's possible that I am experiencing some kind of karma tied to a past life as a Viking, which may be the reason why I am drawn to Buddhist teachings and a peaceful existence but also to learning about ancient barbaric cultures. I feel that we are not meant to fully recall our past lives because if we could, we would not have a pure experience in this one. Maybe the reason we get glimpses, dreams, feelings, and signs, which connect us to our past lives, is to enable us to transcend karmic bonds to grow in each lifetime. It is all very interesting to speculate.

Carpe Diem

I have traveled to Europe several times over the years and felt a strong connection to the land and people in several of the Viking territories, particularly Denmark, Iceland, and Sweden. I visited a Viking museum in Roskilde, Denmark many years ago with my ex on our first trip to Europe together and was very much at home around the ancient artifacts and restored Viking ships. There was a festival happening at the time with entertainment and craftspeople creating replicas of jewelry, weapons, attire, belts, etc. and it evoked a feeling of being transported back in time.

We took a ferry from Copenhagen to Alborg, which is an old Viking fishing village in Northern Denmark, and I felt as though I had been there before. As I walked through the town, I noticed synchronistic signs everywhere such as, *Enjoy life like a rock star*, which is a motto that I have embraced throughout my life. There was a building that had a sign out front with an eagle on it that said, *Spirit of America*, a bar that had a Statue of Liberty wrapped in a flag with a *Manhattan* sign underneath it, and *Las Vegas* signs along one of the streets.

The main square had a giant bull in the center, which had meaning for me as a Taurus. In Egyptology, the Apis bull is a symbol of creativity, strength, and primordial power. I can recall thinking that the phrase, "If you mess with the bull, you get the horns," definitely expressed my personality well as I stood next to the enormous statue.

We happened to be there during the high school graduation period, and the entire country was celebrating. Many of the graduates were wearing captain's hats while being driven around in green busses during the day and partying in the streets at night. They were very proud of their accomplishments, and there was a feeling of community spirit throughout the town. The people genuinely seemed to care about one another.

It was inspiring speaking with the graduates about their future goals and hearing about their excellent educational system. They were intelligent, enthusiastic, and joyful as they talked about manifesting their dreams. I was very impressed with how they valued education and that teachers were highly regarded as a vital part of society. Teaching is considered a noble profession there, and many of the students were aspiring to become educators.

I had a great time visiting Alborg. It truly left a lasting impression on me as I boarded the ferry back to Copenhagen, ordered some wine, and toasted to the town with a traditional Viking toast... *Skol*!

Several years after my trip to Denmark, I visited Iceland during the summertime to celebrate my sister Laura's birthday and invited my friend Jada (wolf totem). We all stayed at a hotel in Reykjavik, which was a lively little city with great shops, restaurants, and bars. We visited some historical buildings such as old churches, checked out waterfalls, craters, geysers, black sand beaches, and bathed in a mineral hot spring called *The Blue Lagoon*. The landscape in Iceland is majestic with its lush green mountains and meadows, rock formations, and stunning coastline. I was in awe of the beauty all around me and felt like I wanted to ride a horse over the miles of untouched, open terrain through the country like I would have done in the Viking days.

A few months before our trip, Jada was a model in a music video for a rock n' roll band. She was so excited about the airing of the video but did not have any information about the date that it would premiere on television. As we were sitting in our hotel room in the middle of Reykjavik discussing it, we happened to turn on the tiny, old tv, which had less than ten channels, when suddenly her music video appeared on the screen... The odds of that occurring were so remote that we were completely floored by the synchronicity and knew the rest of the trip would be magical.

On the evening of June 21st, the summer solstice, I walked along the shoreline as the sun was both setting and rising simultaneously on the horizon, which occurs during the summer months in the Northern Hemisphere. I took a picture of a large sculpture of a Viking ship with the sunset/sunrise behind it, which perfectly captured the essence of living in the present, between past and future..

Later that night, we had dinner at a restaurant that happened to be called *Carpe Diem,* and I truly resonated with the meaning of the words, which is what led me to get the phrase tattooed on my ankle once I returned home. I was greatly inspired by my trip and wanted to continue witnessing the beautiful sunsets around the world in as many countries as I could, before my next incarnation...

Stonehenge at Sunset

A few months after traveling to Iceland, I went back to Europe on a two-week whirlwind trip through England, Italy, France, and Germany with my ex and his daughter. We began the adventure in England, where we were able to book a semi-private tour of Stonehenge in Wiltshire, which is an ancient Neolithic monument with giant vertical stone pillars and horizontal stone slabs across the top called Dolmens. Each standing stone is around 13 feet (4.0 m) high, seven feet (2.1 m) wide, and weighs approximately 25 tons, with smaller stones called Bluestones scattered throughout the site. According to archeologists, it was likely built around 2500 B.C. and is one of the best-known ancient wonders of the world. The weather was perfect when we arrived in the late afternoon as the sun was beginning to set on the horizon, creating a magnificent backdrop. As I circled the giant megalithic stones, I wondered about the people who had placed them there and the reason for doing so. Was it a calendar, a ceremonial meeting place, a portal of some kind? It is believed that a mysterious culture known as the *Druids* built Stonehenge, but that has not been entirely proven. Like many other ancient structures, we may never know the truth about how or why they were constructed.

The energy there was powerful, and I wanted to experience it with no one else around, so I decided to hang back for a few minutes after the tour concluded, and the group headed back to the bus. I sat in the middle of Stonehenge alone and meditated for a short while, which felt like an eternity, as the sun was disappearing behind the giant stones. The impact of that indescribable moment in time was forever etched on my soul.

The Wonders of Italy – Florence, Venice, and Rome

We traveled from England to Italy and stayed in Florence, Venice, and Rome visiting as many historical buildings, museums, and monuments that we could fit into each full day while dining on fabulous Italian cuisine. I was on sensory overload between the art, music, architecture, and ancient ruins such as the Pantheon and Coliseum.

As I walked through the cobblestone streets of Florence, I thought about the fact that Leonardo da Vinci (1452–1519) and Michelangelo Buonarroti (1475–1564), along with many other genius artists, had walked the same streets during the Renaissance, which was a period in history marking the revival of classical art and literature. The masterpieces produced in the region were so spectacular that it is considered a very significant and sacred time in the history of Europe.

The marble sculpture of David created by Michelangelo was breathtaking, and I thought of his quote, "Every block of stone has a statue inside it, and it is the task of the sculptor to discover it. I saw an angel in the marble and carved until I set him free."- Michelangelo. It has always reminded me that a potential masterpiece lies dormant in raw materials until the great mind and technique of the artist brings it out into the world.

We arrived in Venice in the middle of the night and took a gondola ride along the canals to our spectacular hotel. It felt wildly romantic being there, and I was soaking it all in as I imagined what it must have been like centuries ago. We only had one day to spend in Venice, so the following morning we visited St. Mark's Square, which is a famous landmark and center in Venice and often referred to as the "Church of Gold" due to its' opulence. There were crowds of people enjoying the ambiance, musicians playing a variety of instruments, and artisans selling crafts. It was a great way to start our morning in the city.

Later that day, we visited the Murano Glass Factory, which had quite an interesting history. Apparently, in 1291 AD, the glassmakers of Venice had to move to the island due to the threat of fires. They established a thriving community of glass artisans there, which still exists today.

The store at the factory featured beautiful glass sculptures, vases, chandeliers, bowls, and other assorted items. My favorite piece was a blown glass guitar that was very impressive in both design and craftsmanship. We were able to see a glass blowing demonstration in the same studio where generations of artisans have been doing so for centuries, which fully enriched our experience there.

After our brief visit to Venice, we traveled to Rome and arrived late in the evening once again. It was challenging finding our hotel between the confusing streets and the language barrier. We finally made it there, completely exhausted, but looking forward to seeing the Vatican, Coliseum, Pantheon, and other sites in Rome.

The following morning we visited the Vatican Museum, which displayed priceless artifacts from around the world, and I wondered about the Vatican Library. It was not open to the public, and only certain individuals are allowed to enter the private rooms, as they contain a multitude of ancient texts and other items. It reminded me of the Alexandria Library from ancient Greece, which housed the world's most sacred documents and was burned to the ground in 48 B.C. It is believed that some of the scrolls were spared from the fire and may be contained in the vaults of the Vatican. Lucky are the few who have been granted access to the secret archives.

The Sistine Chapel in the Vatican Museum contains frescos along the walls and high ceiling with scenes from the bible. Michelangelo painted it over four years while he hung, sometimes upside down, from scaffolding. I stood beneath the magnificent masterpiece and felt overwhelmed with admiration. The entire composition was breathtaking and must be viewed in person to be truly appreciated.

The Coliseum was an impressive feat of engineering, indicative of the ingenuity and power of the Roman Empire. It was built in 70-72 A.D. by Emperor Vespasian and was opened for entertainment purposes by his son Titus in 80 A.D.

As I sat in the stands where the crowds of people would gather thousands of years ago to view the gladiator and animal fights, I thought about the fact that history has been replete with blood-thirsty games and entertainment. Over 3,500 years ago, the Mayan civilization held ball games where the participants were brutally sacrificed by having their chests ripped open and their beating hearts removed and then consumed by the powerful rulers. Bullfighting, which originated in Spain around 711 A.D., has been a part of their cultural tradition for centuries. The blatant disregard for the sacredness of life throughout history has been the darkest aspect of humankind since the first act of killing for means other than survival.

Although the Coliseum was an incredible structure, the intention behind it made me think about the fall of Rome and every other civilization built and maintained through greed, war, bloodlust, and tyrannical rulers such as the Emperor, Julius Caesar (100-44 BCE). He was the dictator of the Roman Empire until he was killed by assassins, some of whom were trusted members of his Senate. It seems the following phrase backfired in his case, "Keep your friends close, but keep your enemies closer"- Sun Tzu

On our last day in Rome, we visited the Pantheon, which was built as a temple dedicated to all of the pagan gods in 118 A.D. and considered one of the most well-preserved buildings in all of ancient Rome. It felt very mystical walking around the interior with the marble statutes of the gods and the large oculus dome in the ceiling, which was designed to contemplate the heavenly realms.

I have always been interested in Roman and Greek Mythology and the way that the gods, goddesses, and legends were interwoven into both cultures. There is much that modern civilization does not understand about their vital role in the lives of the people who worshipped them. Some scholars believe that higher-level beings may have existed at the time who were more advanced than humankind and considered godlike as a result. This idea is not just exclusive to Greek and Roman gods and goddesses but believed all over the planet in places such as; Egypt, India, Africa, Japan, and many others. I have often wondered if we will ever really know the truth about a large portion of the history of the world.

Germany and the Dichotomy

After our experience in Italy, we traveled to Germany, which was delightful and picturesque during Christmas time, and everyone seemed to be in the holiday spirit. We shopped in the Christmas markets that were set up in all the towns while drinking a famous hot wine beverage called *gluhwein*.

We visited Bavaria in Southern Germany and traveled on a winding road known as *The Romantic Road* while stopping along the way to tour the beautiful castles that were nestled in the idyllic countryside. The scenery was breathtaking with the beautiful lush landscape and snow-capped mountains all around, and it felt like a fairytale setting.

The next day we decided that it was important for us to visit Dachau, which was the first concentration camp that Hitler had built in the year 1933 as the model for the other camps which he had systematically constructed throughout Germany and Poland.

We arrived at Dachau in the late afternoon, and there were hardly any people walking around. As we entered the gates, there was a guard tower across from the entrance, the prisoner's barracks to the left, and the Nazi officer's headquarters to the right. A long, abstract horizontal metal sculpture that looked like barbed wire with people twisted throughout it like trapped souls was placed in front of the officer's building. It was a haunting reminder of the depravity and horrific violence that human beings are capable of enacting.

I could sense the agony, despair, and death as I walked around the camp at dusk in the frigid cold, but I also felt a glimmer of light in the darkness as I thought of those who continued to hope and pray for a miracle. There were many incredible acts of bravery and compassion among the prisoners, which helped sustain them until the Allied troops finally liberated the survivors at the end of the war. Several of my ancestors were killed in Nazi Germany, and I imagined what it must have been like for them to suffer so needlessly. I thought about the fact that if I had been living in Germany or Poland back then, I too might have suffered the same fate. Dachau was a dark and depressing contrast to the castles I had visited the day before, and I was overwhelmed with such a feeling of sadness after being there that I went back to the hotel and wrote a poem;

Man's Inhumanity
Evil
The Soul measured
Light
Night
If only tortured Souls had wings
They could have flown away
Very far
Evil sinking
Would drown in deep remorse
Doomed. - Susan Ross

The following day after the challenging experience at Dachau, we visited an amusement park that was culturally themed with many different attractions and rides. It was a complete dichotomy to the concentration camp, and I was trying hard to process what I had experienced in Bavaria, Dachau, and then the vibrant park.

As I walked around the magnificent attractions, I felt the dark, cold, heavy energy from the camp start to dissipate in the warmth of the sunshine, and the phrase Carpe Diem came to mind once again. I had the realization that I was lucky to have been born in a place and at a time where I was not under the control of a brutal regime, and I felt grateful to be alive and free.

The Palace of Versailles, France

We traveled from Germany to France and visited several spectacular cities and towns, including Niece, Cannes, Avignon, Toulouse, Bordeaux, Versailles, Normandy, and then Paris for New Years' Eve. We booked a tour of The Palace of Versailles, where Marie Antoinette (1755-1793) was crowned the Queen of France and then later beheaded for her role in bankrupting the country.

The palace was opulent and extraordinary with rooms and hallways that were lined with gold and a magnificent garden, which was meticulously crafted with trees, blooms, fountains, and statuary.

Marie Antoinette's life story epitomizes the greed, wastefulness, and corruption that occurs when impulse overrides intuition and reason, sometimes to the detriment of the masses. She was a young and inexperienced girl from Austria who was wedded to King Louis XVI of France in 1770 A.D. in an arranged marriage and given control of ludicrous sums of money, which she spent on extravagant and frivolous things. There was no one guiding or restricting her, so she did what most young girls would do after being given that much power and wealth without direction. She purchased expensive items, threw lavish parties for all of her friends, and ruinously caused a collapse in the economy of France. It has been said that she responded to the outcry from the people of France by saying, "Let them eat cake," indicating that she could care less about the damage she had caused.

In a karmic twist of fate, she paid the debt with her life as she and the King were captured by angry citizens while attempting to escape on the same road she had traveled to the palace on her way to becoming the Queen of France. They were both later tried, convicted, and beheaded by guillotine for their crimes.

The Queen's story is a reminder of how greed and excess can cause so much devastation, which has been the case throughout history. She was so young and given so much money and control all at once that it is not surprising she behaved the way she did. Her life was an example of the freedom of choice and the damaging, sometimes deadly repercussions of poor decision making. "We reap what we sow."- Apostle Paul

Omaha Beach, Normandy

The following day we traveled to the northern region of France to Omaha Beach in Normandy, which greatly impacted me as I felt both sadness and gratitude thinking about all of the brave people who died for the freedom that I enjoy every day. I walked along the shore where the Allied troops defeated the Nazis in the Battle of Normandy, referred to as D-day, on the morning of June 6th, 1944, and imagined the courageous soldiers who fought for their countries and the world. If they had not defeated Hitler's army on that day, and he succeeded with his evil plan, many more people would have perished, and the world would be quite a different place today. I stood in silence as I looked towards the ocean and honored them with a salute for their incredibly selfless service to all of humanity.

Later that afternoon, we visited the Normandy American Cemetery and walked along the perfectly lined rows of white crosses, Jewish stars, and other headstones with the lush green grass all around. I was moved by how the cemetery was beautifully laid out to pay tribute to the brave souls whose bodies lay beneath the surface.

The Bayeux Tapestry

After the cemetery, we visited a small museum in Bayeux, Normandy, to view the Bayeux Tapestry, which is an intricately embroidered work of art nearly 231 feet long and almost 2 feet tall. It depicts the events leading up to the Norman conquest of England, culminating in the Battle of Hastings in 1066 A.D. I had learned about its' existence in an art history class in college and had always wanted to see it in person. The entire tapestry was displayed in a small museum and set up to be viewed from the beginning of the story to the final battle scene. It documents the events of yet another battle fought for power, land, riches, and religion.

As I viewed the exquisite masterpiece and tried to take it all in, I reflected on the fact that history repeats itself through both war and peace, which have been in a constant state of conflict since the dawn of civilization. I decided not to focus my attention on the negative aspects of humanity, but rather the courage of the many people throughout history who have triumphed and flourished. I was deeply affected by all that I had seen during my journey and the incredible talent, creativity, and ingenuity of the human race.

Mont Saint Michele

I was excited about our next excursion to a castle in Normandy called Mont Saint Michele because of a synchronistic experience that had taken place about a week before my trip. I happened to be surfing through some television channels late at night and decided to watch a movie called *Mindwalk*.

The film began with a conversation between two old friends, one who was a politician who just lost the election for the presidency of the United States and the other who was a famous writer and poet. They were driving along a winding road with a large impressive building that looked like a castle up ahead of them in the distance. When it came into view as they approached, I realized that it was Mont Saint Michele, the site that we were planning to visit in Normandy... I had never seen or heard of it until I researched things to do and see there and decided to visit and book an overnight stay in a room on the premises. The film explores political, social, scientific, and spiritual topics in a dialogue between two men and a woman during the entire movie while they are walking the grounds.[20]

The castle was initially called Mont-Tombe in the 8th century and has served as a strategic fortress, prison, and place of pilgrimage for centuries. It became known as Mont-Saint-Michele after St. Aubert, bishop of Avranches saw a vision of Archangel Michael, who guided him to build an oratory there as a focal point of the castle.

Archangel Michael is believed to be a loving angel of protection who was chosen by the creator to watch over humanity in some esoteric belief systems. As a result of the bishop's vision and the sacred oratory, it rapidly became a beacon, attracting people from all across the world for centuries. After seeing the film and learning about the history of the site, I was looking forward to visiting there.

I was beaming with excitement as we traveled the same road I had just seen in the movie as the castle was coming into view in the distance. When we finally arrived, we entered through a gate and walked throughout the magnificent rooms, the chapel, and around the winding passageways. The architecture was impressive, and the different areas had both dark and light energy as they had been used for a variety of purposes, some quite disturbing, throughout history.

After touring the castle and having dinner at a lovely restaurant on the grounds, I decided to walk to the top, towards the golden statue of Archangel Michael. I navigated the circular pathway under the moonlit, star-filled sky in a reflective state after being exposed to so many different places and emotions during the trip, and I thought about the synchronicity of watching the movie right before visiting Mont Saint Michele. The brilliant conversations in the film regarding the nature of reality, the cosmos, and what is truly important in life inspired me, and I was spellbound that I was there at that moment.

I walked to the very top and decided to sit and ruminate on the things I wished to address in my life. I had been enjoying a wonderful, decadent lifestyle for many years and was very grateful for everything, but something was missing that I couldn't articulate. I can recall thinking the words, "I just want to go camping." That simple sentence was a life-changing epiphany. I realized that I needed to simplify my life and embark on a spiritual journey once I returned home. It felt as though I had received some divine inspiration from Archangel Michael that evening.

New Year's Eve on the Champs Elysees in Paris

We arrived in Paris two days before New Years' and planned to attend a party at the *Musee de l'Homme* (*Museum of Man*) for New Year's Eve. We spent some time at the Louvre Museum, and I was on sensory overload as I viewed the art I had only seen in books. I felt like I needed several days to enjoy everything, but we were on a tight schedule, so we had only a few hours to walk through the entire museum. I was able to view Leonardo da Vinci's *Mona Lisa*, which was definitely on my art "must-see" list as well as many other priceless artifacts and paintings. I was awed by the talent and genius of the artists, and very thankful that their masterpieces have been so well-preserved throughout history.

The following day we strolled around Paris, visited the Eiffel Tower, shopped at the boutiques, and ate chocolate-filled croissants. We enjoyed the New Year's Eve party later that night while watching the fireworks light up the sky over the Eiffel Tower and the main street through the city called the *Champs-Elysees*. I felt much gratitude and excitement as I celebrated the New Year with a new perspective.

Expansion

My trip to Europe took me on a voyage through my soul, and while I was processing the entire experience, I thought of the story of Buddha and realized that I too was having a similar existential crisis. I began delving into metaphysical subjects such as Sacred Geometry, Ancient Mystery Schools, The Kabbalah, The Kybalion, Yoga, The Emerald Tablets, Eastern Philosophy, etc. I read countless books on a variety of topics and recognized that the symbols and ideas that I was learning about had been a part of my life even before I knew what they meant.

I recalled what the Council of Elders had said about me being a "Symbologist." I felt as though I was being guided to discover the sacred teachings that have been kept hidden for centuries. The mind-expanding wisdom that I was piecing together like a puzzle was captivating as I began seeing the sum of the parts as the whole story; that science and spirituality were intertwined.

Summer in Sweden

My ex and I had parted ways a couple of years after my transformative trip to Europe, which is when I began visiting countries around the world on my own. Although I was becoming less materialistic, I needed to be more financially stable and wanted to continue traveling, so I went back to school to earn credits above my Master's Degree. I was able to support myself and take trips by making pivotal choices and sacrifices. I became accustomed to a different way of living that was enabling me to connect with myself on a deeper level, and I had some incredible realizations as a result. My self-confidence increased as I continued to travel on my own and I was learning a great deal from each place that I visited.

I returned to Northern Europe once again as I was enrolled in a class at a university that offered an opportunity to earn credits abroad by participating in a unique summer program for teachers from the school district. Our professor, Dr. Spangler, was an accomplished musician and performer who enabled high school students from both Florida and Sweden to get together for three weeks to create a musical from scratch based on a chosen theme each year. He named it *The Lovewell Academy,* and the teachers were invited to assist the students in the creative aspects of the musical.

When my group arrived in Sweden, we met in Stockholm and spent time visiting museums of Viking artifacts, shopping, and dining. The following morning we traveled by bus to a town called Oskarshamn, where we stayed for the duration of the program.

We had our first class that afternoon, and I was astounded when I looked at the syllabus. A book that I had just finished reading about synchronicity called *The Spontaneous Fulfillment of Desire: Harnessing the Infinite Power*, written by Deepak Chopra, was a part of our suggested reading list for the course...[21]

After I got over my initial jolt of excitement, I listened intently to Dr. Spangler as he explained the concept and began telling us a personal story about an experience he had with synchronicity right before he arrived in Sweden. A friend was driving him to the airport and gave him a postcard that had fallen from a book she found that morning. It had an image of Atlantis on the front, and she said that she felt compelled to give it to him for some reason. He told us that whenever he facilitates the program in Sweden, he arrives at the location, not knowing the theme that the students have chosen. Once he discovered that the theme for that year was Atlantis, he understood why he was given the postcard.

I spoke with him immediately after class about the fact that I had read Deepak's book right before my trip. We were both intrigued by the synchronicity of my having read a book about synchronicity, which led to a synchronistic experience... I looked forward to learning from him and was eager to see what *The Lovewell Academy* was all about.

The teachers who participated taught a variety of subjects such as Music, Art, English, and History. We all got along well and helped the students with creative ideas for clothing, stage set design, music, etc. but we mostly observed the kids in action. They were very impressive as they wrote the entire storyline and all of the music over three weeks in both English and Swedish. At the end of the allotted time, they performed their musical called *The Drop* for the public in a small theater in Oskarshamn, which was truly special.

I was fortunate to have been able to participate in such a fabulous program while also visiting Sweden and having fun. As part of our assignment for the class, we were required to create a project about our experiences, so I chose to design a collage that was very sentimental to me, as it included many of my great memories.

My travels throughout Europe most definitely sparked my desire to explore many other parts of the world. I was inspired by the beauty, history, art, and diverse cultures that I had seen and couldn't wait to pack my bags once again and fly to another country.

When I was a young adult, I was always drawn to other cultures and enjoyed learning about their history when it was taught through storytelling. I had certain teachers throughout my life who were able to bring history to life and others who would generally write facts on the board to be copied into a notebook and memorized for a test. I did not learn much from routine memorization and was bored to distraction. The teachers who told great stories were always my favorite, as they inspired me to want to travel and learn about the world. Now I have my own stories...

Chapter 5
Love & The Grateful Dead

The Boy in the Bandana

I believe that I may have fallen in love for the first time during the summer before entering high school with a boy I met when I went RV camping with my family in Nashua, New Hampshire. My older sister Laura and I were walking through the campground one early evening, and we passed by a group of boys sitting around a campfire. They said hello and asked us if we wanted to join them for a barbecue because they had a lot of food. We were thrilled that they invited us and went back to our campsite to get permission from our parents to join them. Their site was right next to ours, so my parents were okay with it. The boys were hilarious and cool, and I quickly developed a crush on one of them. He was a rugged, handsome eighteen-year-old with longish brown hair and wore a bandana around his head. They played the music of the Grateful Dead while sitting around the campfire drinking beer, laughing at each other's jokes, and cooking on the grill. They described a Dead Show as an experience not to be missed and that my sister and I should make sure that we see them someday. That night was my first introduction to the Grateful Dead, whose music later became a major influence in my life.

After a fun night, the boys asked us if we wanted to go hiking with them up Mt. Washington the following day. Of course, we said yes but had to get permission from my parents again. Things were different back then, and the boys were likable and respectful, so our parents agreed to let us go. The boy I had a crush on drove me in his truck while playing a hypnotic song by The Dead, as they have often been referred to, called *Fire on the Mountain*.[22] The song and memory were imprinted on my soul, and I recall the feeling I had whenever I hear it. We had a great day hiking and built a bonfire in the evening at the campground once we returned. I had never felt such a strong attraction to a boy before and was not too sure how to handle it. I could tell that he felt the same way about me, but due to the age difference, he kept his distance and was very respectful the entire time.

On the last day before my family planned to head back home to New York, my sister and I went paddle boating with the boys on a lake by the campground. My crush and I were alone on the paddleboat and I was having trouble with the foot pedal. He moved my foot into the proper position, and I felt a bolt of electricity go through me that was so intense that I flinched, and he apologized. He then went on to say that it was so frustrating for him that I was only fourteen because he had such strong feelings for me but could not act on them due to my age. He respectfully took my hand in his and kissed it gently while I blushed bright red and felt like I was going to pass out. My heart was beating like crazy, and my chest felt like it was going to explode as I sat there, unable to speak. He said that he would always think of me once we parted ways and that maybe one day we would see each other again when I am older. At that moment, my sister was standing by the dock and said that my parents wanted us back at the campsite for dinner. I was actually relieved that I had time to process what had just happened, so I said goodbye to him and that I would see him later.

When my sister and I went back to the boys' campsite in the evening, they informed me that he had an emergency at home and would hopefully be back the following morning. Well, he was unable to return the next day, and we never got the chance to say goodbye. As my family and I hit the road in our RV, my heart was aching with each long mile back to New York. It felt like I was being pulled further and further away from him, minute by minute. That was my first experience with love lost, which also taught me a great deal about life.

My Wild Heart

I entered high school after that summer, which I enjoyed for the most part, but I couldn't wait to graduate and spread my wings. I was a devoted fan of Stevie Nicks, whose talent is extraordinary as both a solo musician and the lead singer of Fleetwood Mac. I listened to her albums, *Bella Donna* and *Wild Heart*, over and over again, as well as the numerous Fleetwood Mac albums.

She was a rock goddess, and I wanted to be just like her, so I dressed in gypsy clothing and dyed my hair blond. My last words in my high school yearbook were the lyrics to Stevie Nicks' song *Wild Heart*, "Don't blame it on me, blame it on my wild heart."[23] - Stevie Nicks

SUSAN ROSS

"Don't blame it on me, blame it on my wild heart." — Stevie Nicks. Swimming; Band. Art.

It was my "wild heart" that led me to my first Grateful Dead concert when I was a 17-year-old high school senior, as I had a special connection to them because of my experience in New Hampshire. I decided to attend my first show at RFK Stadium in Philadelphia in 1986 with a friend, and I can recall driving up to the parking lot and seeing all the colorful people, cars, vans, and buses with the music of The Dead playing all over the place. I couldn't wait to jump out and experience the magic that I sensed was there. People were selling all kinds of unique jewelry, clothing, and an assortment of other items, and everyone was having a great time.

As I was walking through the lot, I spotted a beautiful young girl with long dark hair dressed like a gypsy selling sparkling beaded jewelry. She was holding two black velvet boards with some of the most enchanting earrings, necklaces, and bracelets I had ever seen. I approached her immediately, and she introduced herself as Carla. I complimented her on the jewelry and bought a pair of purple and turquoise earrings. We talked for a while, and she was excited that I was seeing The Dead for the first time as she recalled her first show as being life-changing. She very confidently said that she would see me in the future, and she was right about that.

I went into the concert wearing a new tie-dye shirt to match the beautiful earrings and feeling more excited than I had ever felt before in my life. The energy was heightened, and the fans were thoroughly enjoying themselves even though the band hadn't hit the stage yet. It was a balmy summer day after raining all morning and was the perfect temperature as the sun was setting over the amphitheater.

Suddenly, a rainbow appeared in the sky over the stage like it had been planned, and everyone began cheering at nature's display above our heads. A man was walking through the crowd with a very young child on his shoulders who had long blond hair and big blue eyes. She looked like a little angel as she was wearing a crown and waving a wand with a golden star on the end of it. She reminded me of the lyrics to the Beatles song, *Lucy in the Sky with Diamonds*.[24] I watched the man carry her through the crowd as she was touching people with the wand, and I was mesmerized by the effect she seemed to have on everyone. The whole scene was surreal and seemed totally out of the realm of ordinary existence. The man brought her over to me, and as I looked into her eyes, she touched the top of my head with the star wand. I felt a surge of energy travel down my spine and throughout my body as the band started playing the first song of the evening at that exact moment. The entire crowd of thousands of people began dancing, and my body moved in perfect rhythm to the music. People speak of intense spiritual and religious events as life-changing, and it was such an experience for me. I didn't realize back then that I had what the ancient Indian Sanskrit texts refer to as a *Kundalini Awakening*, which I will discuss in a later chapter.

The concert was so incredible that my friend and I decided that we absolutely had to travel to the next show. We made plans with some people to meet up with them at Giants Stadium in New Jersey the following day. We drove there from Philly and arrived at the stadium in the early afternoon, which gave us plenty of time to enjoy the parking lot festivities. I ran into Carla again, and she was so happy to hear that I had such a phenomenal experience at my first show and remarked, "See, I told you so." I expressed to her how much I admired her jewelry and asked her how she learned to make such exquisite pieces. She replied that she was mostly self-taught and offered to teach me her techniques at her home not far from where I was living at the time, and I happily accepted.

A few weeks later, I made plans to meet with Carla. She lived in a beautiful estate with her family, where she had her own large living space filled with trays of beads and pieces that she had created. I learned how to make jewelry in an incredible setting, and I am grateful (no pun intended) for her generosity, wherever she may be today. She is the reason why I have been a jewelry designer for over thirty years.

I could write an entire book about the hundred-plus Dead shows that I attended. I met fascinating people, listened to great music, danced for hours, sold jewelry in the parking lot, and even hung out backstage on occasion.

The Grateful Dead changed my life in very profound ways, and I would not be who I am today without the experiences I had while traveling around the country to see them. It is difficult to describe a Grateful Dead concert. You just had to be there to understand.

The Skull Asteroid

Jerry Garcia, the lead singer and founder of The Grateful Dead, died on Aug. 9th,1995. I can remember exactly where I was when I heard the devastating news. It was a tragic day, and people all over the world were mourning the loss. It was the end of an era, and it felt as though the magic was over.

A few years later, like a Phoenix rising from the ashes, the remaining members of The Dead decided to play on, as solo performers and together, often with additional guest musicians, while touring under a variety of different names. I went to a show several years ago where they were performing as *The Dead and Company* on Halloween at the Madison Square Garden Arena in New York City on Oct. 31st, 2015.

There was a fantastic motor home that once toured with The Dead parked on the street outside the arena called the *Peacemaker*. My sister Kimberly and I were invited inside to hang out for a while before the show. After spending time with some great people and reminiscing about the good old days, we decided to stop for a glass of wine on the way to the venue. While I was standing at the bar, I happened to look up at the television and noticed a news flash about an asteroid passing by the earth that looked just like a skull, which is the symbol and logo for The Grateful Dead... If I had not looked up at that moment, I would have missed the remarkable synchronicity.

It was a phenomenal experience being at the concert on Halloween, twenty years after Jerry's transition, as a skull asteroid was passing by the earth. I believe that it was a sign from the cosmos that the music and magic of the Grateful Dead lives on...

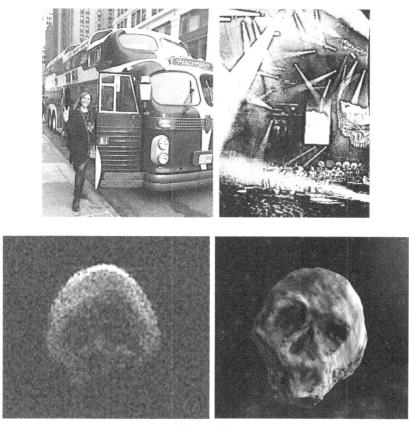

Figure 9

The image on the left of asteroid 2015 TB145, a dead comet, was generated using radar data collected by the National Science Foundation's 305-meter Arecibo Observatory in Puerto Rico (photo by NAIC-Arecibo/NSF). The image on the right is an artist rendering of the comet.

> "Once in a while, you get shown the light,
> in the strangest of places if you look at it right."[25]

> "What a long strange trip it's been."[26]

> -The Grateful Dead

Chapter 6
The Hamptons

The Cassette Tape

After graduating high school, I attended college in the Hamptons in New York, where I met my friend Danielle. When we were both still in high school, we lived in different towns but happened to have a mutual friend named Jody, who suggested to both of us that we should meet because we had so much in common, such as the same taste in music. Jody discovered that we both planned to attend South Hampton College in NY in the fall, and she gave Danielle my phone number to contact me before school began. Danielle never called, but we ended up meeting through synchronicity anyway.

We happened to be in the same art class but didn't realize it at the time. I ran into her one evening at a rock n' roll bar called *My Father's Place*, which was about a three-hour drive from our college campus. A band called *Go Ahead* was playing there that evening, which was formed by members of both the Grateful Dead and Santana. We recognized each other from class and had a quick conversation before returning to our seats.

Once we were back at school, we started hanging out together, and I visited her dorm room one day to find that she had a bunch of cassette tapes with music from bands like Pink Floyd, Led Zeppelin, and The Dead. As I was looking through them, I noticed my name and telephone number were written on the side of a mixed Grateful Dead cassette. I was confused and asked her why she had my name and number, to which she replied that her friend Jody had given it to her... That was when we realized the connection and the coincidence, not knowing about synchronicity at the time.

Danielle and I became fast friends and then roommates during the school year and the summer months, renting apartments or cottages in various parts of the Hamptons each season. It was a popular location for the rich and famous, who came out to play during the summer each year. We went to parties at mansions, shopped like crazy, went to concerts, hung out with famous musicians, attended biker events, and enjoyed life to the fullest. We met all kinds of eclectic characters and had a lot of fun. We worked as waitresses in the evenings and as hostesses during the day for a bus company called *The Hampton Jitney* that transported people from New York City to the Hamptons and back all summer long. We made friends with some of the passengers and got invited to fabulous events and parties, which was one of the perks of the job.

We were lucky to work at a bar on the weekends called *The Hansom House*, which was more like a museum than a bar. The creator and owner, Jon Jacques, was an artist with a PHD in philosophy, and his establishment was a testament to his ideas, beliefs, and talents.

There was a large, quartz, castle fountain outside the front of the bar, and the entrance was like walking through the rabbit hole from *Alice's Adventures in Wonderland,* with an optical illusion hallway and door. The bar had several rooms with cozy couches, unique paintings, incredible stained glass windows, unusual objects, a hansom carriage, and a trippy décor that made one contemplate many philosophical ideas.

Figure 10

I worked in the backyard area where people sat around a bonfire while the Reggae house band played jammin' music all summer long. Everyone enjoyed the artsy vibe, and the place was packed every weekend. There was a secret garden with a rock waterfall in the back of the property behind a fence. It was closed to the public, but we got to hang out there when we weren't working, and it was awesome.

There was even a practical joke in the ladies' room, which had a painting of Michelangelo's statue of David with a protruding fig leaf covering his genitals. If you raised the leaf, a buzzer sounded in the main room to let everyone know you lifted it, which was both hilarious and embarrassing.

Figure 11

Unfortunately, the bar no longer exists as it was sold many years ago and has been completely rebuilt. I am so grateful that I was a part of the happening, and the incredible memories will always be with me.

Figure 12

I also worked a couple of summers as a waitress during the day at a beach club located on a famous strip of beachfront homes called Dune Road. I played beach volleyball on my days off and partied at the various clubs and bars at night. I was living a fast-paced lifestyle, but I managed to maintain a good balance between work and play. I learned a lot of valuable things during that time, which shaped my character in many positive ways.

After attending college and spending summers in the Hamptons for a couple of years, I transferred to Hofstra University in NY to complete my teaching degree. I was fortunate to have an art history professor named Dr. Schwartz, who told incredible stories about different cultures, art, architecture, customs, and beliefs with enthusiasm, suspense, and humor. I looked forward to attending his lectures and even writing the required research papers as they were always based on exciting topics. He was an inspiration to me on my path to becoming an art teacher.

My Calling

My travels, experiences, and exposure to diverse cultures have enabled me to be fearless, confident, and open-minded. I believe that hard work, dedication, and creativity are the keys to success. Every person has a *calling* but must open his/her eyes, ears, and hearts to discover it.

I knew that I wanted to be an art teacher during my first year in college when I was fully immersed in art, and I am still teaching over thirty years later. I have helped students of all ages and abilities to tap into their imaginations to create projects that are meaningful for them. I enjoy seeing the results of their efforts, as well as their pride in their accomplishments.

My classroom is a place of self-expression and exploration, and I learn as much from my students as they do from me. I try to get to know each of them on a personal level, and help them figure out what they are most passionate about pursuing after high school.

I have been blessed with the opportunity to see thousands of teenagers go out into the world and manifest their dreams. It is wonderful when some of them come back to visit and tell me about the great things they are doing in their lives. I know in my heart that I have chosen the right career, and I am grateful to be able to work with young people from each generation to the next.

The following simple quote expresses my teaching philosophy;
 "Art flourishes where there is a sense of adventure." - Alfred North Whitehead

Part Three

Sound, Light & the Cosmos

The Secrets of the Universe

Are Revealed through Vibration

Chapter 7
Sacred Math & Science

"If you want to find the secrets of the universe, think in terms of energy, frequency, and vibration."- Nikola Tesla

Down the Rabbit Hole...
The next two chapters deal with some of the spectacular mysteries of the cosmos. The information presented is based on experience, intuition, and research. I have put together a mosaic of math, science, spirituality, and ancient wisdom that have many different avenues yet to be explored.

I feel as though I have been given mysterious clues that I must decipher and then explain in a comprehensible manner through my interwoven stories and the concepts that I present. The following information you are about to read is complex and multifaceted, so take it in slowly.

It has been said, "When the student is ready, the teacher will appear."– The Buddha

But first, a quick story...

Many years ago, I was involved in a volatile situation with a tenant whom I tried to evict that had a profound synchronistic outcome. He was struggling with his painful, traumatic past and unable to let go of the negativity plaguing his life. Without going into detail, I gave him thirty days-notice to leave my home per our lease agreement. When he refused to vacate at the end of the thirty days, I confronted him, and he hit me several times in the face. I was able to get away and ran to a neighbor's house to call the police. When the police sergeant arrived on the scene and could not get him out of the house, they had to call the SWAT team after I informed them that he legally owned a gun, which was likely in his possession. It was an awful feeling knowing that my dogs were in the house, and there was nothing I could do to get them and keep them safe. My neighbor's young daughter could see how upset I was while the team surrounded my home, and a helicopter was flying overhead, so she sat cross-legged in front of me and started chanting *Aum*. I am not sure that she understood the significance of what she was doing, but it helped me as I prayed to the universe that everything would work out and that no one would be harmed.

At that moment, I heard a woman's voice over one of the officer's radios say, "It's okay; I've got him." She was an off-duty officer with the canine unit who happened to be in the area at the time. He had attempted to flee out the back door when her German Sheppard police dog took him down in the desert, and she arrested him. She came into my neighbor's house to tell me personally that everything was going to be okay, and as she walked towards me, I saw that she was wearing a sweatshirt with a giant *Aum* symbol on the front... I was speechless at first and then thanked her profusely for her role in making sure there was a peaceful outcome. I went home once the awful drama was over, feeling as though some powerful universal force had intervened on my behalf.

Aum and the Sri Yantra

The *Aum* symbol, often spelled OM, represents the entire known universe and all of creation in the Hindu belief system. Aum is considered the primordial sound vibration from the beginning of our universe on to infinity... It is believed that all other subsequent sound vibrations originate from the sound of Aum. It is contained within all forms and connects all things, living and non-living. It has been chanted during spiritual practices such as yoga and meditation for thousands of years to invoke a feeling of oneness.

It is a scientific fact that everything in the universe is vibrating on a particular frequency and contains a unique sound signature. In Hinduism, the concept is known as *Nada Brahma*, which translates to "all is vibration," and the sound of Aum is referred to as the "unstruck sound" and called *Anhad Naad* (Aum of creation).

The *Sri Yantra* is an ancient Indian Sanskrit symbol that is said to graphically represent the sound vibration of Aum involved in the creation of the material universe. It contains the five basic building blocks of matter known as the Five Platonic Solids, which I will refer to later in this chapter. The symbol is comprised of nine interlocking triangles radiating from a central point called the *Bindu* (seed) within a double-ringed lotus mandala and an outer square. The Bindu is considered the seed of the universe, the triangles and lotus petals

---

represent different aspects of creation, and the square represents life on earth and the four directions or doorways to higher consciousness. It is a very potent symbol that is said to bring wisdom, protection, and abundance to those who work with its power for positive outcomes. The word *Yantra* means "instrument of freedom" in Sanskrit, and an assortment of Yantras with specific meanings have been used for centuries as meditation devices.

I was in a heightened meditative state once while listening to the sound vibration of Aum chanting when an image of the Sri Yantra appeared in my mind's eye. I was slowly drawn inside the three-dimensional form and felt as though I was moving through it. I could hear and feel the sound vibrations all around and throughout my body. Although I had seen the symbol before, I was not familiar with the full meaning of it and had little frame of reference for my transcendent vision. My consciousness expanded after the experience, which inspired me to research the Sri Yantra, and I discovered that it is very multilayered in meaning.

It is also known as the *Sri Chakra* in the Hindu White Tantra belief system called *Sri Vidya,* which embodies the feminine aspects of creation. The goddess, *Lalita Tripurasundari,* is considered the cosmic mother who represents the sleeping, dreaming, and waking worlds, and the Sri Chakra is a symbol of her essence.

I was invited years ago to participate in a Hindu prayer ceremony called a *Puja,* which was based on the teachings of Sri Vidya. It was a sacred mantra meditation ritual designed to pay homage to Lalita while invoking her many attributes. It was so beautifully orchestrated that I truly felt the message of the divine goddess; the universe is physically outside of us and spiritually within us.

After discovering the Sri Yantra, I was inspired to delve into many other aspects of the connection between science and spirituality. Science tells us that matter is made up of vibrating atoms that have different frequencies. When atomic particles are drawn together with the same frequency, they create what appears to the naked eye to be a solid form or object, like when separate music notes are harmoniously assembled to create a song, melody, or symphony.

On a larger scale, the Greek mathematician Pythagoras believed that the celestial bodies had their unique sounds and made music throughout the universe. He called the concept, "The music of the spheres."- Pythagoras

There is a branch of science known as *Cymatics*, which is the study of sound vibrations creating visible standing wave patterns. It was developed by a Swiss scientist and doctor named Hans Jenny in 1967 and proved the fact that sound and matter are linked.[27]

When grains of sand or other fine materials are randomly scattered on a surface like a metal plate, and the plate is vibrated with a sound frequency, the grains arrange themselves into patterns. Depending on the different frequencies, the patterns range from simple to complex and often mimic designs found in nature like on the shell of a turtle. The experiment illustrates the fact that sound manipulates matter.

I purchased a *Cymatics Wave Resonator* so that I could view the phenomenon for myself, and it is truly mind-boggling to see the patterns that emerge with the different sound frequencies.

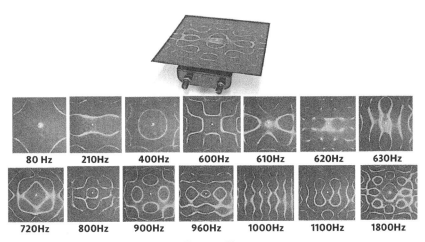

| 80 Hz | 210Hz | 400Hz | 600Hz | 610Hz | 620Hz | 630Hz |

| 720Hz | 800Hz | 900Hz | 960Hz | 1000Hz | 1100Hz | 1800Hz |

Figure 13

Let There Be Light

Another aspect of creation is light. It is scientifically defined as energy in the form of the electromagnetic radiation of a wavelength existing in tiny packets called photons, which are energy particles that have no mass and move at an incredibly high speed. A photon can be thought of as a particle of light and an electromagnetic wave as a light wave. When light is shone through a prism, it refracts into seven rays of varying vibrational energies called the visible color spectrum.

Color is derived from white light, which contains all the colors, and is made up of different frequencies, just like sound. The color red has the lowest/slowest vibration, and violet has the highest/fastest vibration. An object is made up of the color and sound vibrations interacting with one another and coming together as different visible forms. Light, color, sound, and the resulting matter form the structure of our known universe, and the sentient beings within it are equipped with the senses to perceive them.

Through a complex process, the eye is designed to perceive light, color (provided the individual is not color blind), and matter while the ear is designed to hear sound. There is a fascinating connection between the shape of the human eye and the fishlike center shape created by two overlapping circles sharing the same radius known as the *Vesica Piscis*, which is Latin for, "bladder of a fish." It is thought to be a symbol representing the birth canal of the universe bringing forth light in the esoteric branch of mathematics called *Sacred Geometry*. The shape of the eye, which perceives light, and the shape of the center of the Vesica Piscis, which symbolically brings light into the universe, are the same. It is believed, although not proven yet, that the structure of a photon, which is what light is made of, might be the same fishlike shape as well. Another interesting thing about the Vesica Piscis is that it symbolically came to represent Jesus Christ as the *Jesus fish*. Jesus is often depicted with a halo of light around his head, and many of his teachings are centered on light; "Then spake Jesus again unto them, saying, I am the light of the world: he that followeth me shall not walk in darkness, but shall have the light of life" – John 8:12-58

Various representations of Buddha, Hindu deities, and angels are depicted with halos of light around their heads and bodies as well. When one is enlightened, it is said that he/she is vibrating on a high frequency similar to light. The word light has been used to describe a state of being such as light-hearted, a phenomenon during near-death experiences reported by many as seeing a bright light at the end of a long tunnel, and as the phrase "I see the light" signifying wisdom.

"Light is the basis of the Universe. Light is the essence of everything. We are created from light, sustained by light, and return to the light."[28]- Christa Faye Burka.

Sacred Geometry & The Flower of Life

The entire universe is based on the principles of mathematics. In many cultures, numbers have a spiritual component and often appear in esoteric texts and belief systems around the world. Specific numbers and numerical sequences are said to be connected to the higher vibratory realms such as 11 11,144, 222, 333 444, 555 and so on... Many people report seeing them repeatedly on clocks, license plates, signs, during dreams, etc. Numerology is the study of number patterns that are said to represent the spiritual aspects of the cosmos. It has been considered a vital part of ancient wisdom, mythology, astrology, and metaphysical studies.

Sacred Geometry describes the mathematical language of shape, form, space, and the stages of creation through the symbolic diagram of the *Flower of Life* symbol. The image contains nineteen overlapping interconnected circles, which represent the various stages of evolving life forms. The seed in the center, like the Bindu in the Sri Yantra, is the point of origin. It is fascinating to ponder that if the theory of our universe having a starting point is correct, then the entire cosmos containing all of the possibilities of creation may have begun just like a biological seed, which creates each individual life form.

The Seed
Life begins with a tiny seed
Instructions within to complete the deed
The question and quest beguiling man is...
Who wrote the instructions and created the plan?
The answer is somehow contained in the seed
The key to the door is all that we need
Our senses can only tell us so much
About the reality we see, hear, and touch
The Faith of humankind is another story
Belief in a creator of infinite glory
The truth is revealed when we begin to look
Life becomes an open book... – Susan Heather Ross

Initially, the pattern begins with one circle symbolizing the *Creator*, becoming two overlapping circles in the first act of creation. The circles are connected through the center, or point of origin, sharing the same radius, and forming the Vesica Piscis (the birth canal of the cosmos). The symbol also represents the process of cell division with one cell splitting into two cells, then into four cells, and then six cells and on to create life. The first six overlapping circles around the center circle create a pattern called the *Seed of Life*, symbolizing the development of many life forms. Adding six more circles around the perimeter of the Seed of Life for a total of thirteen circles creates the dimensional *Egg of Life*, which symbolizes a multicellular embryo in the first stages of creation and development. It is also referred to as the *Genesis Pattern*, representing the creation story in the *Book of Genesis* from the Bible; "For in six days the LORD made the heavens and the earth, the sea and all that is in them, and rested on the seventh day; therefore the LORD blessed the Sabbath day and made it holy."-Exodus 20:11

Stages of the Seed of Life   **Egg of Life**

Adding another six circles around the perimeter of the Egg of Life for a total of nineteen circles creates the *Flower of Life* with multiple Vesica Piscis shapes within the pattern. The Flower of Life symbol represents the blueprint of the cosmos, containing every atom, molecule, and cell within both organic and inorganic matter. It reveals a pattern called the *Fruit of Life* from which *Metatron's Cube* emerges, named after *Archangel Metatron*, whose name means "Angel of Presence." He is believed to be the archangel watching over and protecting the entire universe.

Flower of Life   **Fruit of Life**

Metatron's Cube contains the underlying molecular structure of all of matter called the *Platonic Solids*. There are five Platonic Solids, which are called the tetrahedron, cube, octahedron, icosahedron, and dodecahedron. They each give structure to both inorganic and organic life forms in various combinations and were considered to be the building blocks of all of creation by the Greek philosopher, Plato, which is also confirmed by the science of chemistry.

The Platonic Solids

Metatron's Cube

The Sri Yantra symbol contains the Seed of Life within its structure as well, and they can be superimposed over one another and mapped along the same lines. The Flower of Life and the Sri Yantra are both diagrams representing the link between light, sound, and matter in the universe. They have appeared as symbols in various places around the world throughout history. It is a mystery as to how ancient civilizations understood these concepts without the aid of modern scientific instruments. The Flower of Life has been seen in China, Japan, Egypt, Israel, India, Turkey, Italy, and Spain. The symbol seems to be burned into the wall with laser precision in a temple in Abydos, Egypt, as pictured below on the left. Although the Sri Yantra is believed to have originated in India, the geometric shape is represented in both the Native American and Peruvian cultures, along with many others. It is also the same shape as the Jewish Star of David, with overlapping upward and downward facing triangles.

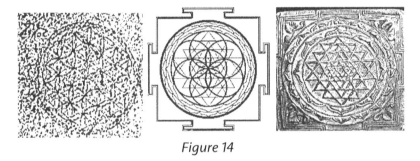

Figure 14

A tapestry of collective, ancient wisdom exists that civilizations have possessed for thousands of years, and there are people around the world who are beginning to realize our infinite potential as we are awakening from a deep sleep. I have been studying and sharing this wisdom with others to be a catalyst for them to seek the truth if they choose to do so. The information is a lens, which can be used to see the bigger picture of creation and humanity's place in the universe.

There have been many prominent philosophers, mathematicians, scientists, artists, sages, and scholars throughout history who have uncovered the many facets of creation and have attempted to teach others what they had learned. They often had to form secret societies to discuss such "blasphemous" concepts and were persecuted when exposed by ignorant, fearful people who controlled and dominated the masses. I am grateful to them all for preserving the knowledge.

Leonardo da Vinci and the Golden Mean

Leonardo da Vinci (1452-1519) was a prolific painter, scientist, and inventor during the Renaissance in Italy. He was very intrigued by nature and the mathematical patterns which seemed to be inherent in all life forms. He did countless sketches of geometric principles, including the Flower of Life symbol, wrote backwards in code, and infused his paintings with Sacred Geometry, which he hid in plain view for fear of being persecuted and possibly killed for doing so by powerful and oppressive rulers. Many intuitive scholars who have studied his work believe that he was attempting to teach humankind the secrets of the cosmos through his sketches and paintings.

Figure 15

Da Vinci's drawing of the Vitruvian Man illustrates how the human body contains a proportion of sacred math, which reflects the ratio between the radius of the moon and earth using simple geometry. The circle above the head represents the size of the moon, and the circle within the square represents the size of the earth. Furthermore, the largest pyramid at the Giza Plateau in Egypt contains the same '51.5-degree angle as the triangle in da Vinci's drawing, which is not random.

Figure 16

Another formula that Leonardo da Vinci was exploring, also hidden in his work, is called the Golden Ratio, often referred to as the Golden Mean. It is known as the *Fibonacci Sequence* or *Phi Ratio,* and it is the mathematical formula of growth for many things in nature, such as plants, trees, seashells, flowers, insects, animals, humans, weather patterns, the pattern of the tides, etc... It is also seen in spiral galaxies embodying the concept, "As above, so below."

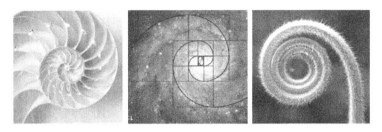

Da Vinci realized that the various parts of the human body are calibrated to the Fibonacci Sequence in relation to one another. He drew sketches of Sacred Geometry and the Platonic Solids as the mathematics of nature, which is illustrated in his sketchbook below.

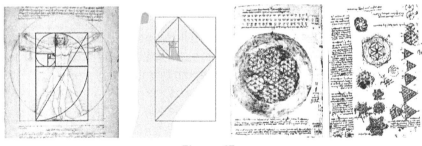

Figure 17

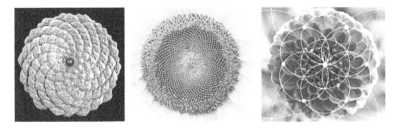

"Learn how to see. Realize that everything connects to everything else."- Leonardo da Vinci

The *Fibonacci Sequence* was discovered by *Leonardo Fibonacci* (1170-1250 AD), who was born in Pisa, Italy. It is an infinite sequence of numbers (1, 1, 2, 3, 5, 8, 13, 21, 34, 55, 89, 144, ...) and each number is added to the one preceding it (1+1=2, 1+2=3, 2+3=5, 3+5=8, 5+8=13...) which creates a logarithmic spiral that grows exponentially larger with each spiral arm. The ratio between any two consecutive numbers is 1:1.618, or the *Golden Ratio*, which is derived by dividing any of the numbers by the previous one. The number will always approximate the ratio 1:1.618, no matter how far the sequence continues towards the infinite. As a geometric expression, it is calculated by reducing a rectangle to a square repeatedly, which creates a spiral.

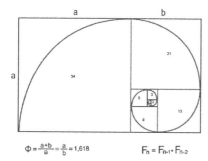

$$\Phi = \frac{a+b}{a} = \frac{a}{b} = 1.618$$

$$F_n = F_{n-1} + F_{n-2}$$

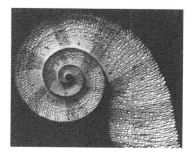

The spiral symbol has been used in cultures throughout the world in pictograph writing such as petroglyphs, art, architecture, ancient stone monuments, etc. since the dawn of civilization.

Many years ago, I visited a 5,000-year-old Neolithic site in Ireland called *Newgrange,* which is a giant rock dome covered by grass. It is surrounded by hundreds of rocks with numerous spirals carved into them, including a large boulder placed at the entrance of the structure. The spiral carvings are thought to represent transformation, life cycles, and the seasons.

Incredibly, the entrance to the site was constructed to align with the sun to illuminate the entire cross-shaped interior during the winter solstice on Dec. 21st, while it remains in darkness throughout the rest of the year.

"The Universe is written in the language of mathematics." - Galileo

It seems that with so many examples of the spiral in cultures throughout history, as well as in math and science, it is a significant unifying symbol of humankind, the earth, and the cosmos. We are living within a giant spiral in our galaxy, spirals are all around us, and our bodies also contain them. I believe that when this concept truly resonates with one on a deep soul level, it is an undeniable, life-changing truth.

The Mandelbrot Set and The Cardioid

The spiral is part of another branch of mathematics called Fractal Geometry. A mathematician named Professor Mandelbrot developed this study of Geometry during the early 1980s by deriving a simple equation, $z_{n+1} = z_n^2 + c$.[29] The fundamental principle of the equation is known as self-similarity, which replicates an infinite number of shapes that are copies of the original one through a process called *iteration*. It is the equation used to describe many patterns in nature, such as trees, flowers, clouds, coastlines, internal organ systems, etc.

The Mandelbrot Set consists of a heart-shaped region at the bottom and a circle at the top with infinite fractal *Fibonacci* spirals extending outward in all directions around the spindly perimeter. It looks somewhat like a seated Buddha and has been called the "Buddhabrot."

  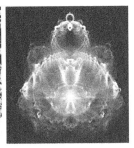

The Mandelbrot Set expresses a mathematical formula of universal creation and has been referred to as, "The Thumbprint of God." It is abundantly clear that math and science provide a language for humanity to understand creation and the order within the chaos.

Professor Mandelbrot came to a profound realization through his mathematical discovery, which is evident from his statement, "My life seemed to be a series of events and accidents. Yet when I look back, I see a pattern."[30]- Benoit B. Mandelbrot

Soon after writing about Sacred Geometry, the Golden Ratio, and the Mandelbrot Set, I had the following synchronicity take place with a good friend and colleague of mine that proved to be quite an extraordinary connection.

Stephanie is a brilliant mathematician and incredible teacher who I have known for the past eighteen years that we have worked together. I was talking to her about my book one morning and discussing the Sacred Geometry chapter with her. She teaches advanced placement mathematics, and her students create various projects throughout the year, which she has displayed around her classroom. I noticed two collage projects hanging on the wall that I realized were connected to the Vesica Piscis. They both contained the equation for the fishlike center shape between the two circles, which I had just written about a few days back. The theme one student chose to represent the equation was a game called *Candyland,* which happens to be my favorite game that I played as a child. The other project featured an image of a spider, which is my shadow/ally totem, and will be described later. They were both very significant signs for me.

About a week after the Vesica Piscis synchronicity took place, I had yet another experience involving Stephanie and mathematics. I was at a gas station before work, and as I was standing at the pump, my attention was drawn to a metal wire shaped like the bottom of the Mandelbrot Set, just lying on the ground. I picked it up because I felt that it was possibly a sign that I needed to investigate further, so I went to Stephanie's classroom to see if she had some mathematical information about the shape and its connection to the Mandelbrot Set. She informed me that it is the shape of a polar equation limacon curve called a cardioid and that she had just taught her students about it the day before in her pre-calculus class. She showed me the lesson in the math textbook, and there was a blank white space above the graph of the shape. I placed the metal piece down on the page in the blank space, and it fit perfectly like a puzzle piece...

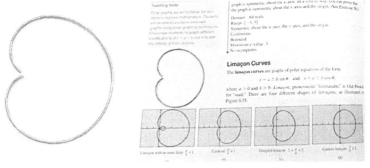

Figure 18

She explained it mathematically but said that she wasn't aware of any real-life applications other than being used in a microphone. I had a feeling that there was a connection between the cardioid and the Mandelbrot Set, so I searched the internet for information.

By definition, a cardioid is a plane curve that is traced by a point on the perimeter of a circle, which rolls around a fixed circle of equal size. There is a mathematical link between the equations, as the Mandelbrot Set contains a cardioid, but I also discovered some other interesting facts about the cardioid. Besides being used for microphone acoustics, it is the equation used to graph the symbol of a heart. Furthermore, cardioids are found throughout nature in the shape of an apple, certain leaves and flower petals, and happen to appear in a coffee cup when the light hits it just right.

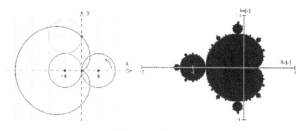

Figure 19

After doing a bit of research and using my intuition, I have realized a profound symbolic and spiritual link between the cardioid and the Mandelbrot Set. The connection is love...

The Mandelbrot Set, containing a cardioid is referred to as the "Thumbprint of God." It also resembles a Buddha (both God and Buddha represent compassion and love). The heart, which is the universal symbol for love, was created by graphing a cardioid equation.

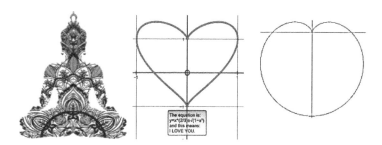

No one knows for sure where and when the heart symbol originated, yet it is present in every corner of the world as a symbol expressing one of the most powerful concepts known to humankind. It is recognized everywhere, instantly, but there is mixed information about how and when it came to represent love.

The word cardioid comes from the Greek word for heart, *Kardia*, and the word cardiac is a term pertaining to the heart in the medical field. There are several theories about why the heart symbol is similar in shape to the heart organ, but no definitive origin has been established.

It is fascinating that as humans, no matter where we are from, it is a common shared experience that we feel love in the area of the chest close to where the heart organ resides. This area is known as the Heart Chakra and will be explained in greater detail in a later chapter.

An apple is in the shape of a cardioid and has been traditionally given to a teacher as a gesture of love and appreciation from a student. The origin of this tradition dates back to sometime in the 1700s, but it is not known for sure how or why it began.

A shadow of a cardioid appears when light hits the inside of a coffee cup just right. Many people all over the world have a love affair with coffee, which has been going on for centuries. There are major corporations that make billions from coffee sales as well as small neighborhood coffee shops that are gathering places for people to socialize. Often coffee is the first thing on many people's minds as they arise in the morning. It is warm and comforting, just like love.

The cardioid appears in many places throughout nature such as in leaves and flowers. It is also the shape of the buttocks on the human body. While I was writing this chapter, I discovered through synchronicity that both a Barn Owl's face and the ancient site of Newgrange, are cardioids as well... It seems that the people who built the site understood the significance of the cardioid as a symbol connected to nature and the cosmos.

  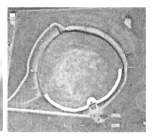

After putting together a symbolic relationship between the two equations, I began reflecting on the age-old question, "What is love?"

In many creation myths and belief systems throughout history, the *Creator* is portrayed as a "Loving God" and human beings as an embodiment and expression of that love. There have been countless stories, parables, quotes, etc. written about all facets of love, such as unconditional, unrequited, undying, forbidden, and the list goes on... It seems that there is a common thread in the many different ideas about love; it is both experiential and immeasurable. It is believed to transcend time and space and is said to possibly link individuals across lifetimes and even across species. Love is present in the animal kingdom and not only exhibited between familial species such as a mother bear and her cubs but also between animals held in captivity from birth who would normally be predator and prey in the wild.

There are two horses, one male and one female, that live in my neighborhood whom I regularly visit as I walk my dog. I noticed that the female was gone one day and didn't see her for several weeks. I was not sure what happened to her, but I feared the worst and thought that she might have passed away. The male horse was all alone, and I could sense utter despair in his demeanor. I tried to comfort him by visiting each day, but he wouldn't come to me as he usually did in the past. One morning I saw that the female horse was back, and the two were standing next to each other looking so happy that my heart was bursting with joy for them. They have not left one another's side ever since and often stand together side by side with their tails moving while comforting one another's faces.

I have been very fortunate to experience love in my life and firmly believe that it can inspire, heal, and create bonds. The feeling of love is not merely an emotional response to another sentient being but a powerful force, which is a part of consciousness that cannot be quantified.

"The secret to living well and longer is: Eat half, Walk double, Laugh triple, Love without measure."- Tibetan Proverb

Love from Above

I was in the process of reviewing this chapter while sitting on my patio under a clear blue, cloudless sky. I was focused on what I was reading but suddenly felt drawn to look up and saw a very distinct image of a heart in the otherwise completely blue sky.

I was utterly amazed...

I feel that I have been receiving signs and messages to guide me on my journey through life but also to inspire others to recognize and explore their own synchronistic experiences. My awareness of the pattern of clues as they appear enables me to derive meaning from the events. It is not a unique gift that I possess; it is a mindset that I believe most people can tap into with a desire to do so. Manifesting synchronicity requires both an observant mind, and an open heart and can transform one's everyday existence into an extraordinary one.

"The unexpected and the incredible belong in this world. Only then is life whole."[31]- Carl Gustav Jung

"I believe that imagination is stronger than knowledge. That myth is more potent than history. That dreams are more powerful than facts. That hope always triumphs over experience. That laughter is the only cure for grief. And I believe that love is stronger than death."[32] - Robert Fulghum

Anahata
(Heart Chakra)

"We are slowed down sound and light waves, a walking bundle of frequencies tuned into the cosmos. We are souls dressed up in sacred biochemical garments, and our bodies are the instruments through which our souls play their music."[33]- Albert Einstein

Chapter 8
Creation Myths and Beliefs

"There is no religion higher than truth"[34]- H.P Blavatsky

The Union of Opposites
There are many different versions of the creation story which express the role of sound, light, and polarity in creation such as in *The Book of Genesis* from the *Old Testament* verses 3-5; "And God said, 'Let there be light,' and there was light. God saw that the light was good, and he separated the light from the darkness. God called the light 'day,' and the darkness he called 'night.' And there was evening, and there was morning—the first day."

According to this explanation, God "spoke" the light into existence and "separated the light from the darkness," thusly creating a system of duality and balance. Without duality and opposing concepts, the universe and all of its contents could not exist. In order to know a *thing*, there must be an opposite *thing* to compare it to, which creates a balance between the two, resulting in a third *thing*. This principle of polarity exists in the atom (protons, neutrons, electrons), temperature (cold, warm, hot) location, (down, middle, up) time, (morning, noon, night), value (white, gray, black), and numbers (negative, zero, positive), and so on. The concept of evil exists in order to know good, and we have been granted the free will to choose between them.

The role of the number three in creating balance in all aspects of the universe occurs in many creation myths and belief systems around the world as well as in science. The triangle, which has three sides and three angles, has been used as a symbolic expression of balance, strength, polarity, and unity throughout history.

In early Christianity, the concept of the *Triune* or *Holy Trinity* (Father, Son, and Holy Spirit) symbolizes the Creator, creation, and consciousness. In the ancient Chinese philosophy of *Taoism*, the Yin Yang symbol represents two opposites (Yin-female, Yang-male) coming together as a third whole, with each side containing a part of the other to create a balance between the two.

The Kybalion

There is a book called *The Kybalion* that was published in 1908 under the pseudonym *The Three Initiates* and is attributed to the teachings of Hermès Trismegistus, the Greek Messenger God whose name means "Thrice Great." He is said to have mastered the three planes of existence; mental, spiritual, and physical. The book contains the profound wisdom of the universe and the concept that "All is mind."[35]

The Seven Hermetic Principles:
1. The Principle of Mentalism
2. The Principle of Correspondence
3. The Principle of Vibration
4. The Principle of Polarity
5. The Principle of Rhythm
6. The Principle of Cause & Effect
7. The Principle of Gender

On the cover of *The Kybalion* are the words, "The lips of wisdom are closed, except to the ears of understanding." - The Three Initiates

The information contained within the doctrine is only for the seeker of the truth and the prepared mind.

"The noblest pleasure is the joy of understanding."- Leonardo da Vinci

Shiva Nataraja

In the Hindu pantheon of the gods, *Lord Shiva* is a part of the trinity comprised of *Brahma (*Creator*), Vishnu (*Preserver*), and Shiva (*Destroyer*). There are different beliefs about the order of importance of each and religious sects that worship one over the others. However, it is understood that all three are part of a *whole* called the *Trimurti.* In the Hindu belief system called *Shaivism,* Shiva is considered the Creator, Preserver, and Destroyer of the universe existing within a state of eternal regeneration. He is depicted with long dreadlocks representing wisdom, a crescent moon on his head indicating his control over time, a third eye on his forehead for insight, and a snake around his neck for consciousness. He holds a drum called a *Damaru* in his left hand to symbolize the vibration of the Universe. In his right hand, he holds a trident called a *Trishula* symbolizing the three aspects of creation (creation, preservation, destruction), the three states of consciousness (sleeping, dreaming, waking), and the three states of being called the *Gunas (Tamas-inactivity, Rajas-activity, Sattva-virtues).*

It is believed that *Shiva* (Creator) merged with an ethereal substrate called *Prakriti* (Creation), and the three Gunas (states of being) that emerged from the union are the essential aspects of energy, matter, and consciousness. The Gunas are always present in all beings and in varying amounts. *Tamas* is a state of darkness, inactivity, and inertia, often deluding people from spiritual truth. *Rajas* is activity, movement, passion, and change and cause attachment, longing, and desire if not kept in check. *Sattva* is virtue, wisdom, and harmony. Depending on one's state of being, the Gunas can either be in or out of balance. Hinduism teaches that it is imperative to rise above the three Gunas to reach *Nirvana* (enlightenment). The Bhagavad Gita, an ancient Indian holy text states; "When one rises above the three Gunas that originate in the body; one is freed from birth, old age, disease, and death; and attains enlightenment" - Bhagavad Gita 14.20

The Dance of the Cosmos

Shiva is often depicted as *Nataraja,* which translates to *Lord of the Dance*, whereby he is standing on one leg indicating the balance (preservation) between creation and destruction within the cosmic dance of the universe. There are two large statues of Shiva displayed at the CERN laboratory in Switzerland where the seventeen-mile underground particle accelerator/collider called the Hadron Collider was constructed to find an elusive, hidden, underlying force field in the Cosmos known as the Higgs Field. The Higgs-Boson particle within the Higgs Field is believed to have given mass to elementary particles such as protons and electrons at the inception of the universe. The physicist Leon Lederman called the Higgs-Boson particle, "The God Particle" in his book, *The God Particle: If the Universe Is the Answer, What Is the Question?*[36]

In 2012, the Hadron Collider detected this particle, which was considered to be a tremendous milestone in the study of physics and the nature of our universe and may have opened a doorway to understanding more about consciousness as well. There are many mysteries yet to be explored and hopefully divulged that could help humanity evolve both technologically and consciously.

The Kabbalah

An ancient text called the *Kabbalah*, also known as the *Zohar*, states that before the universe came into being, there was no space, time, or motion. The only thing that existed was the *Light*, which had no form and nothing else to compare itself to, so it could not know and share itself. It is said that the *Light* created a *Vessel* to share itself with, which became the receiver of the *Light*, in a relationship of giving and receiving in only one direction.

At some point, the *Vessel* wanted to experience sharing and giving, so it pushed back the *Light,* causing what is described as the restriction called *Tzimtzum* to occur, which shattered it into zillions of pieces across the cosmos. The parts of the shattered *Vessel* became all the fragments of matter and energy that make up our entire universe; atoms, animals, people, plants, everything...

The Kabbalah teaches the value of overcoming the ego and being generous through the metaphor of the *Light* and the *Vessel*. It also addresses self-control and not succumbing to constant longing throughout life, which causes suffering, similar to the Buddhist idea of desire and detachment. It is believed that there are many opportunities to transform ourselves by resisting temptation and being positive, which results in allowing more of the *Light* into our lives to be able to vibrate on a higher frequency. It is also important not to get triggered by negative people and events with the idea that being proactive (positive) rather than reactive (negative) will allow us to grow spiritually. The teachings in the Zohar are a guide or prescription for living a life of stability, passion, happiness, and peace.

The Tree of Life

The Tree of Life in the Kabbalah is a mystical symbol containing an arrangement of 10 interconnected spheres called *Sefirot,* which are considered to be divine emanations or attributes of the Creator. It is believed to be a map of the universe and contains the aspects of the Creator and creation through 32 pathways. The 10 spheres are connected through 22 lines or channels joining the energy of each together, which corresponds to the 22 letters of the Hebrew alphabet.

When the Tree of Life is superimposed over the Flower of Life, the Sefirot line up perfectly with particular intersection points within the pattern of the Flower of Life. The center or seed of the Flower of Life and the Sefirot of compassion and creativity called *Tiphareth (*Beauty) on the Tree of Life are linked in their placement, representing both creation (seed) and Creator (compassion and creativity).

The Sri Yantra, Flower of Life, and Tree of Life are connected symbols of divine wisdom. They all line up perfectly with one another when they are layered which indicates that the teachings are linked as well.

There are three columns contained within the Tree of Life. The right column is masculine, luminous, and active, the left column is feminine, dark, and receptive, and the column in the center unifies the two along the spiritual pathways to create balance between them.

The system of the Tree of Life is a comprehensive diagram representing both practical and spiritual concepts in the human experience. It can be useful as a guide for creating a prosperous and meaningful life.

The Sefirot

Central Column
1. *Kether* (Crown) - the Creator
   Daat (behind tree) - hidden mystical state
6. *Tiphareth* (Beauty) - compassion, creativity
9. *Yesod* (Foundation)– knowing, manifesting
10. *Malkuth* (Kingdom) – material, physical world

Right Column
2. *Chokhmah* (Wisdom) - divine revelation
4. *Chesed* (Mercy) - grace, emulation of the creator
7. *Netzach* (Victory) - initiative, fortitude

Left Column
3. *Binah* (Understanding) - repentance, acceptance
5. *Gevurah* (Strength) - intention, determination
8. *Hod* (Splendor) - surrender, sincerity

The Four Realms
The ten *sefirot* are divided into four realms or facets of creation:
Atziluth - the infinite
Beriah - the creative
Yetsirah - the formative
Assiah - the material

The Chakra System

The word *chakra* means "wheel of light" in Sanskrit. Seven main chakras align with the spine, and each one has a specific function and quality. There are also many minor chakras throughout the body, which all work together to help us strive for health, balance, happiness, and well-being. A mind, body, spirit connection exists between the individual chakras as well as both positive and negative aspects of each. When a person is experiencing an issue with one chakra, it throws the other chakras out of balance. Once he/she is aware of the specific qualities of each chakra, he/she can use strategies such as diet, yoga, meditation, being in nature, reading, writing, listening to music, etc. to work through the imbalance and begin the healing process. The chakra system is similar in many ways to the structure of the Tree of Life in the Kabbalah, as both describe various physical, emotional, mental, and spiritual aspects of human existence.

Root Chakra - "I AM" Sanskrit: *Muladhara*
"Support"- Stability, survival, grounded, fearlessness...
Color – red / **Element** - earth
Location – base of the spine
Organs – (elimination) colon, anus, urethra / **Sense –** smell
Issues – instability, feeling lack, fear
Mantra – I am grounded, stable, and protected. (Shanti Hum)
Seed Sound – Lam

Sacral Chakra - "I FEEL" Sanskrit: *Svadhisthana*
"Sweetness"- Joy, abundance, creativity, emotions, passion...
Color – orange / **Element –** water
Location – below the naval
Organs – (sex organs) bladder, prostate, womb / **Sense –** taste
Issues – emotional, sexual, lack of passion and creativity
Mantra – I am creative, joyful, and balanced. (Ananda Hum)
Seed Sound – Vam

Solar Plexus Chakra -"I DO" Sanskrit: *Manipura*
"Lustrous Gem"- Confidence, willpower, motivation, purpose...
Color – yellow / **Element –** fire
Location – between the naval and heart
Organs – (digestive) stomach, gut, pancreas / **Sense –** sight
Issues – low self-esteem, ego, weakness
Mantra – I am confident and manifest my desires. (Dharma Hum)
Seed Sound – Ram

Heart Chakra - "I LOVE" Sanskrit: *Anahata*

"**Unstruck**"- Compassion, unconditional love, generosity...
Color – green / **Element –** air
Location – the chest
Organs – (circulation) heart, lungs, thymus / **Sense –** touch
Issues – anger, poor relationships, isolation
Mantra – I am love, compassion, and gratitude. (So Hum)
Seed Sound – Yam

Throat Chakra - "I SPEAK" Sanskrit: *Vishudha*

"**Purification**" - Expression, communication, truth...
Color – blue / **Element –** sound
Location – the neck
Organs – (endocrine) throat, thyroid, parathyroid / **Sense –** hearing
Issues - poor communication and expression, overbearing
Mantra – I am truth and express myself freely. (Sat Nam)
Seed Sound – Ham

Brow/Third Eye Chakra -"I SEE" Sanskrit: *Ajna*

"**Percive**" Insight, clairvoyance, wisdom...
Color – indigo / **Element –** ether
Location – midbrain
Organs – (limbic system) pituitary/pineal glands / **Sense –** intuition
Issues – spiritually disconnected, lacking insight, negative outlook
Mantra – I am wisdom and intuition. (Aum)
Seed Sound – Aum (lower pitch)

Crown Chakra -"I AM ALL" Sanskrit: *Sahasrara*
"Thousandfold" Oneness, consciousness, enlightenment...
Color – violet / **Element -** consciousness
Location – top of head
Organs – (nervous system) pineal gland, spine / **Sense –** akasha
Issues – depression, confusion, agitation
Mantra – I am one with all of creation. (Aham Brahmasmi)
Seed Sound – Aum (higher pitch)

The lower chakras (Root, Sacral, Solar Plexus) are associated with the physical, material world. They are contained within a downward-facing triangle while the upper chakras (Heart, Throat, Third Eye, Crown) are associated with compassion and spirituality and contained within an upward facing triangle. When an individual has a healthy Root Chakra, he/she feels grounded, stable, capable, and secure. The vital energy contained in the Root Chakra rises through the Sacral Chakra which is the center for joy, abundance, emotional balance, and passionate creativity. This stable, creative energy flows upward through Solar Plexus Chakra, which is the place of action, confidence, will power and manifesting one's goals and dreams. It is like a seed that has been given the proper soil, water, and sunlight to grow and thrive.

When the lower chakras are rotating properly, and in balance, one can begin to experience the spiritual aspects of the upper chakras through the gateway of the heart. The Heart Chakra is the place of compassion, generosity, unconditional love, and gratitude. When a person has a strong Heart Chakra, he/she is vibrating on a higher frequency of love as the energy flows through the Throat Chakra associated with speaking one's truth, kindness in communication, and freedom of expression. From this place of truth, the energy then flows through the Third Eye Chakra, which is also referred to as the all-seeing eye and the *sixth sense* of insight, intuition, clarity, and wisdom. It is located in the midbrain and associated with both the pituitary and pineal glands, which work in tandem to create balance. The pituitary gland has the quality of rational, analytical, reasoning, whereas the pineal gland has the quality of intuition and imagination. The pineal gland perceives light and contains color receptors, a lens, rods, and cones, just like actual eyes. It regulates the body's melatonin, which is its' sensitivity to light and dark, as well as our waking and dreaming states. It forms at the moment of the determination of one's gender, which happens on the forty-ninth day of fetal development. In Tibetan Buddhism, it is believed that after the soul leaves the body at death, it takes forty-nine days for it to incarnate into a new form.

The pineal gland emits trace amounts of a chemical substance called DMT (dimethyltryptamine) throughout one's life and is said to produce the most significant amount of it at birth and death. It is also believed to be involved in some mystical experiences. The famous French philosopher, Rene Descartes (1596–1650) felt that the soul resided in the pineal gland and called it, "the seat of the soul." He believed that the mind exerted control over the brain using the pathway of the pineal gland and that it was a separate entity apart from matter.[37]

Many ancient cultures, such as the Egyptians, have representations of the pineal gland as an integral part of their belief systems. The Eye of Horus is the same shape as the location of the pineal gland within the human brain and contains symbolism regarding the senses.

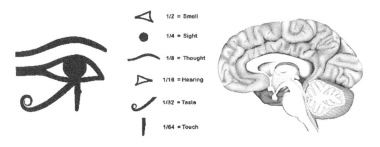

The Third Eye is often represented as a pinecone due to its' similar shape and can be seen as such throughout history. In cultures such as the ancient Sumerians, the pinecone shape was often depicted in the hands of powerful beings, and atop the large staffs that they held in many relief carvings. They may have had advanced knowledge of the link between the pineal gland and consciousness that many other ancient civilizations also seemed to possess. There is even a large pinecone sculpture in front of the Vatican, indicating that the spiritual connection may have been understood and thinly veiled by the Catholic Church for centuries.

There is a link between the pineal gland and the roof of the mouth, which has eighty-four meridian points that are stimulated during mantra chanting, sending the vibrations to the hypothalamus, pituitary, and pineal glands. The word mantra means "instrument of the mind," and reciting specific mantras can lead to higher-level consciousness through the Crown Chakra, which is located at the top of the head. Just as the Root Chakra connects us to the earth, the Crown Chakra connects us to the oneness of the cosmos. It is represented by a thousand-petaled white lotus flower, with each petal acting as a receiver of universal energy, attracting the male energy of Shiva (Creator) down through the chakras.

Each chakra has a certain number of flower petals around its' perimeter when combined, add up to the sacred number 144,000. The petals are stimulated by particular vibrations known as *Bija* seed sounds that are chanted during meditation practice to promote overall well-being. There are many different references to the number 144,000 in ancient manuscripts and scriptures connecting it to enlightenment or being "saved" in some way. I believe that there is a universal truth being expressed through the concepts associated with the chakra system and a powerful energy force known as Kundalini.

Kundalini Energy
Kundalini Shakti (female energy of creation) is believed to lie dormant as stored potential energy below the Root Chakra at the base of the spine until it is stimulated and becomes kinetic (active). As it rises through the chakras to the Crown Chakra to merge with Shiva (male energy of the Creator), it stimulates the petals and elicits a transcendent feeling of heightened awareness. The Hindu tradition describes the experience as a *Kundalini Awakening*, in which a person

has an intense, sometimes overwhelming, feeling that is physical, emotional, mental, and spiritual. I believe that I had a Kundalini Awakening at my first Grateful Dead concert. At the time, I didn't know anything about it, so the feeling was completely raw with no frame of reference. I felt very empowered and blissful, which had a major impact on me, as the experience was a catalyst to search for more magic and meaning in my life.

The ancient symbol for Kundalini is the *Caduceus* staff that is also associated with the medical system as an emblem of good health and well-being. The word Kundalini translates to, "coiled serpent" as it is likened to a sleeping serpent wrapped three and a half times around the sacrum at the base of the spine until it is awakened through a variety of modalities such as yoga, meditation, sexual experience, plant medicine, etc. The number three is symbolic as it represents the states of consciousness (sleeping, dreaming, waking), and the *half* symbolizes the soul.

The central column along the spine containing the seven main chakras is called the *Sushumna*. On both sides of this column are intertwining feminine/masculine channels called *Ida* (lunar/female) on the right and *Pingala* (solar/male) on the left. These pathways transport vital energy through the chakras and the channels throughout the body called the *nadis*, which then transmit it to the *Auric Field* around the body, often referred to as the Eighth Chakra. This field is where we hold the vibration of each chakra and, in effect, the total vibrational frequency we are projecting out into the world.

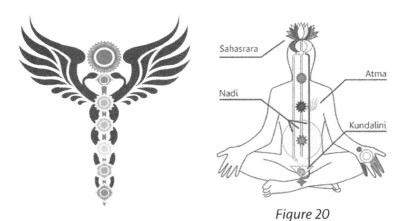

Figure 20

I have also experienced a heightened state while practicing Kundalini Yoga. The *asanas* (postures) are linked together with *kriyas* (movements and chants), *pranayama* (breathwork), and meditation. Two particular *Sanskrit* chants that are associated with Kundalini Yoga are *Waheguru* (sublime teacher) and *Sat Nam* (true name of the Creator). They were designed to invoke the highest level of truth in one's life and foster a sense of oneness with all of creation.

Kundalini Yoga was a very ancient, closely guarded practice, which was only taught by a master to his disciple for centuries until it was brought to the USA by a master from India named Harbhajan Singh Khalsa, also known as Yogi Bhajan (1929 - 2004). He began teaching Kundalini in both New Mexico and California in the late 1960s, as he believed wholeheartedly in the transformative and healing properties of the practice. He took many students under his wing, who later became teachers, and they have taught classes around the world for many years. He founded an international organization called 3HO, which is an acronym for healthy, happy, holy so that people all across the planet could benefit from the wisdom. I was fortunate to have had the unique opportunity to learn a meditation technique from one of his disciples, which I will describe in a later chapter.[38]

Both Kundalini Yoga and the Kabbalah were shrouded in secrecy for centuries and then brought to the public around the same time during a tumultuous period in history. It was the beginning of the *Hippie* generation during which time many people were against the Viet Nam War and tuning in to all kinds of new experiences with sex, drugs, rock n' roll, and spirituality. It was the perfect timing for the receptivity of such life-changing information considering the multitude of people who were making the conscious decision to reject violence, promote peace, and search for meaning.

The wisdom contained in the Kybalion, the Kabbalah, the Chakra System, and many other ancient teachings are similar in many aspects of promoting healing, balance, transformation, and growth. They each offer vital information about consciousness and human development by providing a roadmap to navigate the pathways of the soul.

Part Four

Yoga Retreat Adventures

Create Joy & Balance in Your World

Find Peace in Your Heart & Mind

Chapter 9
Peru

Saksaywaman, Cusco

After studying yoga philosophy for a couple of years, I wanted to deepen my understanding of it in various parts of the world through yoga retreats. My first experience was in the Sacred Valley of Peru at a resort called *Willka T'ika*. I happened to be flipping through a yoga magazine one day, and I saw an advertisement for the retreat, which looked very inviting. The timing was perfect because I was ready for an adventure, so I booked my trip soon after doing some research and contacting the retreat facilitator.

My journey began with a flight to Miami, a long layover of several hours, and then a flight to Lima, which is the capital of Peru. After another layover, I flew from Lima to Cusco, which is a vibrant little city with great cafes, entertainment, sacred monuments, and megalithic rock structures. I met my group at the designated hotel where we would be staying for the evening, and we all got along quite well.

The following day we visited an ancient site while in Cusco called *Saksaywaman*, which is a massive and mysterious three-tiered wall of boulders assembled in rows with the largest one weighing 360 tons at 27 feet high. The stones were cut to fit perfectly together like a puzzle without the use of mortar between them. It was a spectacular feat of engineering, which remains a mystery to this day. The stones in the picture on the right were configured to represent a Llama. It is a sacred animal to the Peruvians and has been an integral part of their culture for centuries.

The energy there was very potent, and I felt completely drawn like a magnet to the magnificent structure. When I touched the giant stones, they felt like they were alive and vibrating. Unfortunately, we only had a short time to visit Saksaywaman, as we were heading to our retreat in the Sacred Valley that afternoon. As fate would have it, I went back there later in my trip and had an incredible experience.

The Sacred Valley

We arrived at Willka T'ika, which was an extraordinary resort in a great location. There were several interesting features and meditation areas throughout the grounds, and I especially loved the colorful chakra gardens. The spacious rooms were beautifully decorated, and the food was grown and prepared on the property.

I spent the first day at the retreat doing yoga, journaling, and relaxing until the evening when I decided to bathe in a tub made of stone in a private garden. As I lay under the expansive sky while gazing up at the multitude of stars in the Milky Way, I pondered the fact that my body is made of the same elements created by them. They are humankind's earliest ancestors, and without them, we would not exist.

I also thought of one of my favorite paintings, Starry Night by Vincent van Gogh. It has been suggested that he painted it to represent how he felt comforted by the stars when he was in the manic phase of his mental illness.

The following quote expresses how he viewed the stars; "Just as we take a train to get to Tarascon or Rouen, we take death to reach a star. We cannot get to a star while we are alive any more than we can take the train when we are dead."[39]- Vincent Van Gogh

Ollantaytambo

The following day after an invigorating morning yoga practice, we visited an ancient site called *Ollantaytambo,* which is a stepped rock structure with rows ascending upward towards the apex of the hill. There were mysterious doorways and rectangular cutouts throughout the site, and the stones were fitted together without the use of mortar, just like Saksaywaman. It was constructed around 1400 A.D. and used as a ceremonial center but was also the site of a major battle that was waged and lost against the Spanish conquistadores.

Around the exterior of the site were perfectly organized irrigation channels allowing water to flow freely through the area, which has been doing so, uninterrupted, for hundreds of years. Some stones were cut with laser-like precision and assembled in a way that suggests a high level of structural engineering was used at that time, which is either lost or remains hidden. One of the features in the irrigation system resembled the geometric outline of a Sri Yantra (Sri Chakra) and is called a *Chakana,* which contains the same root word (Cha) as Chakra. It is an ancient Incan cross that symbolizes the four cardinal directions and the three levels of existence within the Cosmos. The upper world, inhabited by the superior gods is called *Hana Pacha,* the middle world of everyday reality is called *Kay Pacha,* and the lower world of the ancestral spirits is called Urin Pacha. The symbolism of the Chakana and Sri Yantra (Sri Chakra) both express universal concepts.

At the apex of the site, there was a giant megalithic monument made of six boulders weighing fifty tons each within *The Temple of the Sun* that also had an outline of a Chakana carved into the rock face. There were strange protrusions all over the boulders in some sort of pattern or configuration. This type of protrusion patterning can be found in many ancient rock structures all over Peru as well as on other continents. Scholars are still baffled as to their purpose but have many different theories, such as marking particular alignments to the constellations. I wondered how the builders were able to transport the massive boulders up to the top of the hill. Engineers have suggested some possibilities, but there are no definitive answers thus far, and the technology they used remains an enigma.

The features at Ollantaytambo were just as extraordinary as Saksaywaman, and I couldn't wait to visit the famous Machu Picchu, which was next on the list of excursions. My group was fortunate to have a fantastic tour guide who was wise and informative, which greatly enhanced our experience of each sacred site. She had a gift of bringing the magic of Peru to life as she thoroughly explained the history and mystery of the ruins.

Machu Picchu

The day arrived to visit Machu Picchu, and I was thrilled that the weather was perfect that morning. We took a three-hour train ride on a railway called the Inca Rail to the town of Aguas Calientes situated in the Urubamba River Valley, where we reserved an overnight stay. Machu Picchu is believed to have been built in 1450 by the Incas but was hidden from the world until 1911 when Hiram Bingham, a great American historian, resurrected it for the world to experience.

We arrived at the town in the early afternoon and then boarded a bus to Machu Picchu. As we drove along a winding road that was adjacent to the ancient Inca Trail, I imagined all the people who had traveled it over the centuries. I thought about the fact that if I had a lot more time, I would've liked the more authentic experience of hiking the Inca Trail and camping along the way instead of taking the train.

As we arrived at the entrance, the spectacular vision of the ancient structure with the mountains all around took my breath away. The energy there was intense and varied, depending on where I was standing. I felt very grounded in some areas and as though I was lifted to a higher vibration in others. It is not known why Machu Picchu was constructed centuries ago, but like many other sites around Peru, there are numerous theories. It seems likely that it served a spiritual purpose where important events and ceremonies took place.

Although there are some very plausible explanations for many of the incredible features throughout the complex, I found myself relying on my intuition to guide me in trying to figure out the intention behind each area. It was fascinating to explore the possibilities and feel the energy of the stones and the stories contained within them.

Huayna Picchu is the mountain next to Machu Picchu and stands about 860 ft. above it. The Incas built a trail with stairs alongside it and erected terraces in various spots, with the *Temple of the Moon* at the very top. A small group of us decided to see if we could be granted access to climb it, even though the last group for the day was just let through the gate when we arrived. One of the gentlemen in my group convinced the guards to let us through, and we began the very strenuous but exciting hike up the tiny narrow steps and winding pathways to the top. The weather was perfect, and we were fortunate that there were hardly any people around as we made our ascent.

It was a challenging climb, but the reward was worth every step as my senses absorbed the exquisite scenery all around me. It is very difficult to describe the feeling that overcame me once we reached the top and I sat at the highest point of the mountain overlooking Machu Picchu below. It was exhilarating, and I was transformed by it.

After spending some time in the spectacular setting, we made our descent down the mountain and back to the valley below us. It was even more challenging climbing down the tiny steps than climbing up them. We arrived at the exit just in time to catch our bus back to the nearby town where we were staying for the night, and I sat down with the last open seat next to me. When I looked outside the window, I noticed a handsome man about to board and realized that he would have to sit by me. As he took his seat, he introduced himself as Alvarado, and told me that he owned a company that takes tourists on the long trek up the Inca Trail. He had just finished a six-day tour with a couple from Finland that he felt was life-changing for them. I responded that I wished I had hiked the trail instead of taking the train, and he remarked that I would have to book another trip there in the future and that he could be my guide.

He informed me he was a historian of Pre-Incan and Incan studies and proceeded to tell me some interesting information about Machu Picchu and other sacred sites around Peru. He commented that I was visiting Peru at the perfect time because there was a sacred ceremony happening in Cusco the following weekend called the *Festival of the Inti Raymi*. It is held every year to honor the venerated sun god *Inti* during the winter solstice in the Southern Hemisphere.

As luck would have it, the day the festival was being held was a day in our itinerary where there weren't any planned activities, so I could do whatever I wished. I also wanted to spend more time at Saksaywaman, which happened to be where the festival was taking place. When I told him that, he suggested that we meet there, to which I agreed.

We arrived back at Aguas Calientes, and my new friend and I decided to get together later that evening at a local bar where he gave me a fascinating history lesson on the various cultures and beliefs throughout Peru. I felt as though I had just finished reading an entire book on the subject. It was getting late, so we called it a night and agreed to meet for breakfast at a cafe the following morning, where he said that he wanted to show me something special.

I met him at the quaint cafe as planned, and he requested a table by a large window overlooking a beautiful rock formation. As we were having breakfast, he told me that the locals feel that it is considered a sacred structure because it looks like a giant owl was carved into the rock face. He had no idea about my connection to the owl, and that was the special thing he wanted me to see...

He was very intrigued when I told him that the owl was my life totem and a brief version of my experiences. He informed me that in Peru, the owl is a symbol of wisdom, good fortune, and connection to the afterlife. We also discussed the sacred Condor bird, which is associated with the Peruvian sun deity and symbolizes good health, justice, wisdom, and leadership. He had a wealth of knowledge about the spiritual beliefs of the Peruvian people and I was transfixed by the information he was sharing with me. After another great conversation, we finished breakfast and said goodbye until we would meet once again in Cusco.

Pachamama

One of the days during the week, my group took a bus trip on a winding dirt road high up into the Andes mountains to visit a small community of local Quechua people who had recently built a school.

The Quechua have endured a very tumultuous time in history when the Conquistadors conquered Peru during the 1500s, and the survivors retreated to the Andes mountains to hide from the invaders. They settled there once the invasion was over and proceeded to build communities high up on the steep hills where the climate is conducive to farming and agriculture. There have been generations of families living in the mountains and practicing the old traditions and way of life throughout the centuries to the present day.

I was very excited to visit the school, meet all the children, and see what they were being taught. When we arrived at the site, the children welcomed us and walked each of us into their school while holding our hands. Their smiling faces seemed to have a wise, ancient quality to them even though they were young children, and some were beautifully dressed in the traditional Peruvian attire.

They were joyful, playful, friendly, and pure. I felt fortunate to be invited into the beautiful community and was impressed by their ability to do so much with very few basic materials.

The classrooms were vibrant, and the walls were filled with the student's drawings of the mountains they refer to as the earth goddess, *Pachamama*. They have a very sacred connection to nature and the mountains they call home. They recycle everything and use cut plastic bottles to hold school supplies and line the pathways of their campus. They were learning to value and respect the environment.

They performed some traditional songs and dances for us with total enthusiasm, and one of the boys had made a guitar out of cardboard, which he simulated playing during the performance. There was a ceramics class in session that day, which was a real treat for me. We spent the morning with the children, observing their daily routines, and taking photos. They loved having their pictures taken, and I got some great shots that make me smile whenever I look at them.

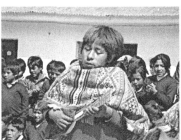 

At lunchtime, the elders were preparing the meals consisting of a potato, a piece of cheese, a piece of fruit, and milk. While the potatoes were being heated in a fire pit in the ground, I wandered over to an area where there were cages of guinea pigs and remarked that when I was in elementary school, we kept them as classroom pets too. Unfortunately, to my dismay, these guinea pigs were not class pets, but a source of food for the Quechua, and I decided to keep my vegan mouth shut at that point.

The children had very few material possessions and used what they had to live simple, happy, fulfilling lives in harmony with *Pachamama*. I was humbled by the experience of being in their presence. They reminded me that the most important things in life cannot be bought or sold and that living joyfully in the moment brings inner peace. When it was time to leave, the whole community got together by our bus and waved goodbye.

Pottery and Pisco Sours

Later that afternoon, a couple in my group that I got along with informed me that they were going shopping at a pottery store in *Urumbamba*, which featured a famous potter in Peru named Pablo Seminario, and invited me to join them. Of course, I said yes right away, and we headed out soon after. We arrived at the store and wandered around, admiring the beautiful pieces. I bought a ceramic owl wall hanging, and they purchased some ceramic tiles.

After we spent over an hour at the shop, they asked me if I would be interested in finding a nice restaurant in town to get a bite to eat and have some cocktails. The manager of the store overheard us talking and told us that her brother owned the best restaurant in the area but that he was usually closed on Mondays. She asked us to wait while she called him to see if by chance he was open and as luck would have it, he decided to be open for a few hours, so we took a *mototaxi* (three-wheeled vehicle), to a restaurant called *Cocina Novo Andina*.

I could tell that it was a special place as the owner, who was a friendly and charming man named Ricardo, greeted us at the door. He invited us inside the restaurant like it was his home and made us a delicious Peruvian drink called a Pisco Sour. The conversation flowed as easily as the drinks, and after a few of them, he said he was going to have his chef make us a spectacular dinner. He closed the restaurant to the public and then joined us at the table. We were served a seven-course meal with incredible vintage wine from his cellar, and he refused to accept payment, saying that we were his guests, so we made a deal with him and paid for a portion of the decadent feast. He was a true gem of a human being, and we were very grateful for his generosity.

We thanked our wonderful host for such a memorable experience before heading back to the retreat for the evening, as I needed to rest up for my next adventure. I was excited to visit Saksaywaman once again and was looking forward to enjoying the sacred festival with my new friend.

The Festival of the Inti Rymi
The following day I headed back to Cusco to meet Alvarado and was both nervous and excited as I boarded a little caravan. I arrived there in the early afternoon and met him at a restaurant that was Bob Marley themed. It was a great place to get together as I am a big fan of Marley, but also because of the synchronicity of meeting him at Machu Picchu while wearing a Bob Marley t-shirt. We ate some Peruvian cuisine and drank Pisco Sours while listening to Reggae.

Cusco was packed with people from all over the world who were there to see the Inti Raymi festival. I was thrilled to be there at such a special time with someone who could translate for me. The energy was vibrating sky high as people began to make their way to the sacred site of Saksaywaman. Alvarado took my hand as we weaved through the crowd to get to a great location to view the amazing spectacle.

Some of the people in the procession were the descendants of royal ancestry dating back hundreds of years, and they were brought onto the field throughout the ceremony to pay homage to the sun god *Inti*.

Symbolic performances were happening all around while hypnotic Peruvian music was playing from large speakers that were strategically placed for optimum sound. The acoustics of the three-tiered ancient rock wall of Saksaywaman created a reverberating sound effect, which added to the mystical experience.

The incredible ceremony was ending as the king was carried onto the field by his people. He rose from his throne on the platform with his arms outstretched towards the sky and chanted a sun-worshipping prayer to the god Inti in *Quechuan.*

Suddenly, as if by his divine will, the clouds parted, and the sun's rays shone through the sky, illuminating the sacred site all around... The entire crowd was astonished and burst into applause at the remarkable phenomenon we had all just witnessed.

The excited people began dispersing and Alvarado took my hand and led me to an area that was like being backstage at a rock concert. The security officer would not allow us access until he said something to him in Spanish that made him change his mind. As we walked among the descendants in ceremonial dress, he asked for their permission to take some pictures of me with them, and they happily obliged.

In the photo below, I am offering coca leaves to a princess in a gesture of respect and vitality. The coca leaf is considered spiritual and medicinal, and it has been an essential part of Peruvian culture for centuries, so it was an honor for me to be able to participate in the ancient custom of sharing the leaves.

As we were leaving the area, I sat on the prop of the King's throne, and Alvarado took a photo of me wearing a cowboy hat that a tourist from the USA put on my head like a crown.

We decided to go into the town to grab some drinks and check out the music scene. The little city of Cusco was jam-packed with people from all parts of the world feeling energized after the intense ceremony. We went to a few different places and had a lot of fun until it was time for me to leave. I thanked him for my extraordinary experience and wished him the best in life. I enjoyed my time with him immensely and was glad that he was my guide. We agreed to keep in touch through email, and he invited me to join him on one of his Amazon rafting tours or Inca Trail hikes in the future. We hugged goodbye, and I boarded the caravan back to the retreat, feeling like I was floating on air.

The rest of my stay in Peru was both relaxing and reflective, as I walked the grounds of the retreat surrounded by the lush greenery and flower gardens. On the morning of our last day, I had a coca leaf reading done by a Shaman who was considered one of the most powerful medicine men in the region.

Shamanism has existed since the beginning of humankind and is deeply rooted in a connection to the earth through plants, herbs, minerals, and universal consciousness. A Shaman is chosen through various signs and challenging initiation rites to be a healer and community leader of the people. He/she is responsible for the well-being of each member of the community and is highly respected for his/her gifts, protection, and contributions.

As the Shaman laid out some sacred objects and coca leaves, he told me that *Pachamama*, the earth goddess, holds me in her arms and that I would return to Peru one day in the future.

Huk Ratukama - See you soon...

Chapter 10
Guatemala

Ashtanga and The Yoga Sutras

After my magical experience in Peru, I found my next adventure
abroad when I was researching information about a style of yoga called
Ashtanga on the internet. I noticed an advertisement for an upcoming
New Year's yoga retreat in Lake Atitlan, Guatemala, at a resort called
Villa Sumaya. Ashtanga Yoga is a practice that incorporates an ancient
doctrine called the *Eight Limbs of Yoga* or *Eight Limbed Path* that was
developed over 1,700 years ago by a man from India known as
Patanjali. The modern *Vinyasa* style practice of Ashtanga Yoga was
developed by a man from India named Pattabhi Jois (1915 - 2009), who
popularized and taught the practice for many years around the world.

The Eight Limbs or steps teach a process for living a meaningful, joyful
life filled with purpose and serve as guidelines for moral and ethical
conduct, self-discipline, and one's physical and spiritual health. It
contains the *Yoga Sutras*, which are 196 Indian Sutras (threads) on the
theory and practice of yoga, and are considered to be a pathway to
enlightenment.

Yoga Sutras

Yamas – environmental attitudes and ethics
Niyamas - self-reflective attitudes and virtuous behaviors
Asana - physical postures as a moving meditation
Pranayama - restraint or expansion of the breath
Pratyahara - withdrawal of the senses and awareness
Dharana - single-pointed concentration
Dhyana – meditation and inward reflection
Samadhi – total integration and unification with the Divine[40]

I wanted to deepen my understanding of The Eight Limbs of Yoga and
the practice of Ashtanga, so I signed up for the retreat, booked my
flight, and headed to the southwestern area of Guatemala. Once I
arrived at the village, I took a boat across the lake to Villa Sumaya and
was greeted by the facilitator and the other friendly participants.

My room was great, and my roommate was a young woman from Australia, who was very pleasant. My group practiced yoga in a beautiful studio overlooking the lake and meditated in the mornings on the dock, which was both serene and energizing.

DNA and the Akashic Field

There was an older gentleman at the retreat who had a powerful presence and was a practitioner of Kundalini Yoga. He told me a story of how he was taught the practice by Yogi Bhajan in the late 1960s in San Francisco after returning from the Viet Nam War. He was one of his disciples for many years and lived with him on an *Ashram* (spiritual retreat) in India. He was an interesting man with a wealth of knowledge, and he led some of the night time meditation sessions. During one particular evening, he brought us through an intense meditation using a Third Eye connection to the Eye of Horus and the largest pyramid on the Giza plateau in Egypt. I felt a doorway open that sparked a desire to know more, and I had a fascinating conversation with him the following day.

As we were sitting at breakfast, we began talking about spiritual topics, and I asked him what he thought about the prophecy of the Mayan Calendar. He explained that as we shifted from the Age of Pisces into the Age of Aquarius over the past few decades, the earth moved further into the photon belt and that we are currently bathed in ethereal light. This light has been helping to activate certain frequencies, which often lie dormant in our DNA, much like the sleeping serpent of Kundalini Shakti. He continued to discuss the idea that our DNA is connected to the *Akashic Field*, which I mentioned in an earlier chapter to be a record of everything in the entire cosmos, including all actions and thoughts. It is believed that this activation is helping humankind to ascend spiritually to a higher plane of resonance and existence. He explained that specific individuals are able to hold this higher frequency more readily than others and have been chosen to assist those who are experiencing difficulty with the vibratory field due to a variety of reasons resulting in anxiety, depression, and anger. The idea was compelling, considering the vast differences in the emotional and mental state of many people today. However, as is the case with some metaphysical concepts, much of the proof is not quantifiable and often too abstract and intangible for most to grasp.

"Few people have the imagination for reality"[41] - Joanne Wolfgang von Goethe

My group and I went on excursions to the neighboring villages around the lake, and I enjoyed them all. We took a boat ride to a weaving museum, a hike to the top of a volcano, and a bus trip to a local market where people exchanged the produce they grew on their farms. We also went on a tour of a small town where the people had few material goods, but some of the best smiles I've ever seen, just like the Quechua in Peru.

A group of young boys was having fun just gathering wood together while a young girl was happily washing dishes in a tiny living space with no electricity and a small wood-burning stove. They all worked together as a community, and I could tell that they took pride in their

tasks. They reminded me once again that happiness is a state of being and that even routine chores can be enjoyed.

New Year's Eve, the Sunset, and the Mayan Calendar

On New Year's Eve, I was invited up the mountain to a dome-shaped building with a small gathering of people from all over the world. When the clock struck midnight, we all held hands underneath a giant glass dome roof and sang 'Auld Lang Syne' in all different languages as the night sky was filled with stars and fireworks.

I had taken some photos and noticed glowing orbs of light floating all around the space in some of the images. Orbs are a phenomenon in photography, which are scientifically and spiritually mysterious, with no definitive explanation as to why they appear in certain photos and not in others. I have seen them in some pictures that I have taken over the years and am always amazed by their appearance. I visited a bird sanctuary once and took a photo of an owl that had a very distinctive orb above its' head and a patch of darker feathers over its' heart. It was a barn owl, which is associated with spirit beings in many cultures.

The following evening, I was practicing yoga on my balcony as the sun was setting over the lake, and there was a beautiful palm tree in front of me. I am fascinated by palm trees and their ability to grow to heights that seem to defy gravity with their narrow but incredibly sturdy trunks. I decided to create a tree pose yoga sequence to express the symbolism of the tree, which I still practice today. I designed it to embody the importance of rooting and grounding while reaching out into the world to learn, grow, and become wise. Yoga teaches valuable concepts that are both inspirational and practical, and I have learned a great deal through my research and experiences.

Towards the end of the retreat, a Mayan Shaman came to the property to perform an ancient ceremony where he blessed us with good health and abundance and read each of our individual Mayan Galactic Signatures. When the Shaman gave me my reading, based on my birth date, I received the confirmation that I was a healer, and that I would use my words to inspire people and help them heal from old karmic wounds. That truly resonated with me, as I had already been doing so throughout my life.

I enjoyed my time in Guatemala immensely, and I felt rejuvenated with the inspiration to continue on my path of having adventures while acquiring wisdom through the lens of a global citizen.

Chapter 11
Brazil

Plant Medicine

A few years after my trip to Guatemala, I began researching a variety of plant medicines used in Shamanic healing. Shamanistic medicine is one of the most ancient ways of healing on the planet and is still practiced today in various countries around the world. Many modern prescriptions are initially derived from nature and then synthesized and watered down for marketability and profit. Some are designed to create a dependency on them and do not actually cure the disease but rather mask the symptoms to make a person feel better while using them. There are often side effects of these medications that can cause depression and even death, depending on the person's body chemistry. While there are pharmaceuticals that are necessary and life-saving, sometimes dietary changes can replace prescriptions such as the case with type two diabetes and certain heart-related diseases. It has been proven that a plant-based diet with the elimination of meat, wheat, and dairy can revolutionize a person's health. There is a great book written on the subject called, *How Not to Die*, by Dr. Michael Greger.[42]

During a healing ceremony, a Shaman is shown special combinations of plants, vines, and herbs to heal illnesses through visions brought on by ingesting certain natural elixirs. One such plant medicine elixir is called *Ayahuasca, Aya* for short, and is a potent combination of both a plant and a vine. The plant contains the molecule Dimethyltryptamine (DMT), which is the same molecule that is thought to be emitted in trace amounts from the pineal gland (third eye) in humans and some animals. The vine is said to turn off the switch that is responsible for producing stomach acid so the DMT can be disseminated throughout the body. The plant is considered female, and the vine is male. In many ancient traditions, the plant has several leaves that are separated by the women of the tribe or community while they bless each leaf with positive affirmations. The vine is hammered and split apart by the men while they chant powerful healing mantras during the preparation ritual. Both the plant and vine are combined and layered in simmering water for many hours until a thick brew similar to tree sap is the final result. It is then consumed by the shaman and other participants in the ceremony.

There are many traditions and practices with *Aya* that people who are seeking wisdom and healing can experience in Mexico, Costa Rica, Peru, and Brazil, as well as other parts of the world. It is a very sacred ritual that can be incredibly transformative, but it can also be a very challenging process for people who have had trauma in their lives. However, it has been said that once the traumatic event surfaces, it can then be dealt with and is often healed.

It is not advisable for people with certain medical issues or mental disorders to use Aya as it can also interact negatively with certain medications. Like many other avenues of powerful medicinal protocols, research is an important part of the decision to participate in a ceremony, and a plant-based, dairy, wheat, and gluten-free diet should be consumed for at least a month before ingesting it.

After reading about Shamanism and plant medicine in Brazil, I chose to learn more about it through an organization called *The Church of Santo Daime,* founded by a man known as Mestre Irineu in the 1930s. Their motto is "Harmony, Love, Truth, and Justice," and the religious practice of the church is based on a blend of varied belief systems that are brought together to promote important life-changing spiritual values.

The word *Daime* means "give me" in Portuguese, and the ceremonies are centered on the premise that the experience will give the initiate what he/she needs, not necessarily what he/she wants. I felt that it was best to participate in a ceremony while being immersed in nature, so I booked a plant medicine and yoga retreat in Brazil, and I flew by myself, not knowing any Portuguese, to a town called Salvador on the Southern coast.

Salvador, Brazil

Salvador was a great little town with a culture known as Afro-Brazilian, which is a combination of African and Brazilian influence.

It was a bit rough with the language barrier, but I managed to explore the town, eat at a restaurant, and shop where I found two shirts that ended up being quite synchronistic during the latter part of my trip. One shirt had an image of Buddha and the mantra *Om Mani Padme Hum* across the top. The other shirt had an image of *Ganesha*, the Hindu elephant deity, with the mantra *Om Gum Gunapataye Namaha* (I will explain what they both mean later in this chapter). I also bought a wire sculpture of a guitar player from a street artist that he said was Jimi Hendrix, which was the only thing he said that I understood. The song by Jimi Hendrix called, "Are You Experienced?" has always resonated with me as I feel that experience is necessary for growth.[43]

I stayed in Salvador by myself for about thirty-six hours until my group arrived to meet up before heading to our destination in Bahia.

The program facilitator was a very personable and intelligent young man from England. He had been studying with a Shaman in Bahia, Brazil for a few years, which was where the retreat would be held for part of our journey. The rest of my group was an eclectic mix of people from all over the world, including New York City. We all got along right away as we boarded our bus in the middle of the night and headed out to *Chapada Diamantina,* which was a pristine forest that was a government-protected site due to the presence of diamond mines in the area.

The first location that we arrived at had charming cottages around the property, beautiful trees and flowers, and a wonderful yoga and meditation area. We stayed there for a few days, practiced yoga in the mornings and evenings, and went on excursions to waterfalls and special places during the days.

There were at least four different waterfalls with fresh drinkable water, and the plumbing systems in the homes and businesses were hooked up to them as well. They were so relaxing that it was difficult to leave once I found my perfect spot at each one, and I felt like I was being purified as I drank the pristine water.

The next place we stayed was in the forest with rustic little cabins throughout the property. We learned about a few plants that were indigenous to the region, as well as the ancient practice of Ayurvedic medicine from India. Some of the plants, such as an Aloe Vera plant called *Tabebuia Impetiginosa,* were said to cure major illnesses and conditions, including diabetes, heart problems, intestinal issues, anxiety, depression, and the list goes on...

While I was there, I met a young seventeen-year-old girl named Amanda, who was passing through town on her way to Rio de Janeiro. She rode her bicycle over two thousand miles from the middle of the jungle in southern Brazil with dreams of attending a university in Rio to become, of all things, an art teacher... She was making money to pay for her travels by creating and selling beautiful dream catchers. Her backpack was filled with balls of string, and she would go into the forest to find sticks that she tied together to create them.

A dream catcher is a Native American symbolic craft with an interior circular design that is woven like a spider web and often contains beads and feathers. They are used as spiritual devices and hung on the wall above one's bed to filter good dreams from the bad ones. They have become quite popular all over the world, as I have seen them in many countries that I have visited. I also teach my students how to make dream catchers in my design crafts class, so meeting her was quite synchronistic all around.

She stayed with our group for a couple of days, and I learned a great deal about survival from her. She was an intelligent, creative, and tough young lady, and I hoped she was able to follow her dreams once she ventured onward to Rio de Janeiro.

My group and I went on a pretty treacherous hike to a waterfall deep in the forest one afternoon. I took a risk to get a picture of me sitting at the top of it, and I'm lucky that I did not injure myself in the process. It turned out pretty good, so I'm glad that I was able to have a reminder of that moment.

The townspeople of Bahia trade produce by transporting it to one another in wheelbarrows through the streets, and they recycle their plastics in woven baskets for pick up along the roads. I found a great Indian restaurant where there was a tapestry of Shiva on the wall and had a lovely conversation with the owner, who was also the chef. I felt that she and I would have been friends if I lived there.

The Sweat Lodge and the Shadow Totem
A part of the retreat involved participating in a sacred sweat lodge ceremony in the middle of the forest, beginning at sunset. The purpose of the ritual is for healing, strength, gratitude, and transformation while releasing toxins to purify oneself physically, spiritually, emotionally, and mentally. I had participated in sweat lodges in the past and knew what to expect. It can be quite challenging and uncomfortable as you sweat profusely, and it is difficult to breathe until you are able to create a rhythm with your breath.

I described the process to my group because none of them had ever taken part in one, and I told them that they have to "tough it out" when it gets rough. Before the ceremony, we sat in a circle and talked about what animals or insects we feared the most. When it was my turn, I immediately said that I had a fear of spiders, as I had a pretty bad case of arachnophobia. It was my shadow totem, which is the creature you fear the most, and when you face it in a vision, dream, or in-person, it becomes your ally totem and protector. Other people in my group had similar insect fears, and we all remarked that ironically, we were in the middle of the Brazilian forest, which was home to some of the creepiest and deadliest insects on the planet.

About an hour before sunset, we headed out on the path through the forest to the *hogan,* which is a small igloo-shaped dome representing the womb of the earth. We prepared the space by making offerings of positive energy with flowers while chanting a beautiful mantra as the stones were being placed on a roaring fire to heat them fully for the ceremony. A mantra can be a powerful word, phrase, or sound vibration that is chanted to invoke healing, compassion, protection, good fortune, etc. and is a potent way to call upon the Hindu deities.

Om Namah Shivaya
Om Namah Shivaya
Hare Kundalini Om
Om Mani Padme Hum
Om Shanti Om
"Salutations to Auspicious Shiva
Remover of all suffering
The jewel in the Lotus of the Heart
Peace"

In the dark of night, we entered the hogan, one by one, saying the Native American prayer *Aho Mitakuye Oyasin*, which means "all my relations" as we bowed at the entrance. We crawled on our hands and knees from the left side around to the right as there was no room to stand. I was the third person to enter and took my place cross-legged with my back against the canvas wall but was still very close to where the hot stones were to be placed during the ceremony. My group finished filing in, and the Shaman took his place at the opening of the flap. We began chanting loudly and playing instruments as the stones were being piled in the center only a few at a time so we could acclimate to the intense heat. I was having a hard time at first but then created a calming rhythm with my breath, and I was in the zone.

All of a sudden, out of nowhere, I felt a giant spider jump on my shin and latch its legs around my calf... I was completely paralyzed with fear when I realized what was happening but knew I had to remove it before it bit me with its' venom.

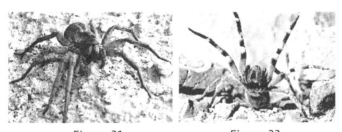

Figure 21   Figure 22

In that frightening moment, facing my shadow totem, I felt an incredible surge of courage as I grabbed its' huge body off my leg and hurled it onto the red hot rocks without hesitation. I was in a confined position where I couldn't move and wanted more than anything in the world to get the hell out of there but knew that if I panicked, everyone, including myself, would have gotten severely burned. The chanting and instruments were so loud that most of my group had no idea what had just happened. The two gentlemen on either side of me, one from Ireland and the other from New York, saw the sparks flying after I launched it onto the stones and asked me what happened. All I could mutter was "Holy F#%@!!! Spider!" The man from Ireland's response was priceless when he whispered in my ear, "tough it out." I crouched my arms and legs together so tightly to try and make myself disappear because I started imagining that there were likely more spiders all around the space. I attempted to stay calm, but it was a major challenge as I was sweating uncontrollably and having difficulty breathing due to the trauma. I focused on an image of Ganesha, the Hindu elephant deity (son of Shiva) and the mantra *Om Gum Ganapataye Namaha,* which translates to "salutations to the remover of obstacles" as I pictured myself getting through the ceremony without further incident. About five minutes later, the Shaman opened the flap of the hogan and asked us if anyone needed to leave. I raised my hand right away, in addition to five other people, while the rest of the group moved out of the way for us to crawl out one by one. With each placement of my hands and knees, I envisioned landing on a friend or relative of the spider that I had just slaughtered. As I was making my way around the circle towards the exit, all I could say to my friends whom I coached to "tough it out" was the word "spider" like a crazy lady. Although I exited the space before the ceremony was over, I felt like a powerful warrior as I emerged from the terrifying experience.

My group and I had to find our way back to the retreat through the forest in pitch blackness with one headlamp between us lighting the way. We were dripping with sweat and grateful to be out of there, especially after I told them about the spider. One of the locals said that it was most likely a deadly, Brazilian wandering spider as there were many in the area. I was overwhelmed by the realization that I could have gotten bitten and died. I discovered later on that it is actually in the *Guinness Book of World Records* as the deadliest spider on earth (I'm not exaggerating, it's true).

Once we arrived at the main area of the building, I saw one of the women from the group had stayed behind and asked her why she backed out at the last minute. She proceeded to tell me that the hogan was covered in plastic to keep the rain out, but when it heats up to high temperatures, it can produce toxic chemicals such as Dioxin. She made the decision not to participate in the ceremony but didn't know if she should tell the group of her concerns and possibly ruin it for us. I could understand her dilemma. I wouldn't have participated either if I had thought about the plastic as well as the fact that deadly spiders were common in the area. I was totally exhausted, so I said goodnight to my group went back to my sleeping quarters for the evening.

After that harrowing brush with death, I pondered the significance of facing my shadow totem in the most challenging way possible and had a synchronistic realization... The spider may have protected me from breathing in toxins from the plastic, as I left the ceremony early, and it was sacrificed to become my ally totem. Furthermore, the shirt I had purchased in Salvador with the image of Ganesha, the remover of obstacles, was a sign that I would call upon him during my journey and that he would come to my aide, which he most definitely did.

The Ceremony under the Gabriel Tree
The following day we traveled to the next retreat, where the Shaman lived with his wife and son. It was a simple brick building in the middle of the forest by a beautiful stream where they created a sacred space under a canopy of trees. Although the Aya ceremony was going to be performed in Portuguese, our facilitator was our translator throughout the trip and was going to guide us through the meditation.

I was immediately attracted to an area in the circle by a beautiful giant Palo Santo tree and set up my comfortable space underneath it. Palo Santo trees are considered both medicinal and sacred. The tree produces a special healing oil, but not until approximately six years after its' natural death. The oil is harvested from the fallen branches and used to alleviate many ailments, including depression and anxiety. The wood is often burned much like Sage to clear discordant energies in an area, and the smoke also has healing properties.

There was an altar by the tree with an offering of seashells. It had a cross behind with a smaller horizontal piece added to the top of it. I was told that the smaller one represented the mind, and the one below it symbolized the heart and was larger to indicate that the heart is more powerful than the mind.

I have always been very drawn to specific trees since I was a young child as they are not only pleasing to look at but symbolic of many things. One of my favorite childhood books is *The Giving Tree* by Shel Silverstein. The story is about the friendship between a young boy and a tree that gives of its apples, leaves, branches, and trunk until the only thing it has left to give is a stump for the boy to sit on when he visits the tree as an old man. It is a lesson in giving and receiving, just like the Tree of Life metaphor in the Kabbalah.[44]

I was astonished to learn that all of the trees in the ceremonial circle were named after archangels and that the one I chose was *Gabriel*... The Shaman's wife gave birth to their son under the tree and named him Gabriel as well. At that moment, I knew that I was being guided and felt a surge of inspiration.

A week before my trip, I had watched the movie *Soul Surfer,* which is based on a true story in which a young female surfer is attacked by a shark and loses one of her arms. The incredible strength and passion of this remarkable young lady, who made a brave comeback by getting back up on her board and winning a major surfing competition, was very inspirational. It also turned out to be a synchronistic lesson.[45]

While reclining under the canopy before the ceremony, I noticed that a large branch on the tree was cut. Suddenly, a stream of sap started running down the limb like it had been wounded and was bleeding. It impacted me, deep in my soul, as a message of strength, perseverance, and fearlessness. The tree was able to thrive even though one of its main branches was cut off, just like the surfer. I felt that it was a message for me to explore during the ceremony and I prepared myself for the internal dialogue .

I felt empowered as the Shaman began chanting after the participants ingested the elixir, while our facilitator translated with his lovely British accent. I drifted into an expanded state of consciousness and felt an incredible sense of gratitude and total compassion as my Heart Chakra opened like a lotus flower.

I reflected on how fortunate I was to have such amazing people in my life as well as my good health, career, and ability to manifest my desires. I felt grounded and connected to Gaia (mother earth) as if she lived within me. My soul became a ball of light and joyously moved throughout my entire body, feeling delighted to be there.

I opened my eyes after a while and gazed up at the powerful Palo Santo tree above me and thought about how strong and majestic it was even though it was wounded. I had an overwhelming sense of connection to all things and felt compelled to rise and wander through the forest. As I walked among the trees to a clearing, I found myself surrounded by brilliant colorful hummingbirds feasting on the flowers all around me in the surreal and magical setting. I felt elated by their presence, as the hummingbird has been a message totem throughout my life as a reminder to be joyful and live in the moment.

After a while, I walked back to my space and sat down while listening to the sacred songs called *Icaros* that the Shaman and his wife were singing. I was in a blissfully peaceful state as the ceremony concluded after a few hours, and it left me with a lasting feeling of tremendous gratitude and creative inspiration. I felt like I had been wrapped in a warm blanket on a chilly day, as I even had one wrapped around me, and was moved to hug my *Giving Tree*.

I just happened to be wearing the Buddha shirt during the ceremony that I bought in Salvador with the mantra *Om Mani Padme Hum,* which translates to "Jewel in the Lotus of the Heart," and I fully resonated with the meaning through my heart-opening experience. I had been chanting *Om Mani Padme Hum* throughout my trip, which was a synchronistic, full-circle connection to the mantra.

Om Mani Padme Hum

Om is the primordial sound vibration of creation.
Mani means jewel and symbolizes the path of nurturing the strongest and richest qualities of the mind like the cultivation of a diamond.
Padme means lotus and is a symbol of the path to enlightenment.
A lotus grows from the muddy waters into a beautiful flower resting above the water. An enlightened mind is similarly capable of rising above an environment that can be challenging (muddy) and blossoming with compassion and wisdom.
Hum represents the unity between knowledge and wisdom.

The Shaman's wife was a *Reiki* healer and did a chakra balancing session with me by the stream after the ceremony. *Reiki* is the practice of transferring universal healing energy to an individual's body and soul through the chakras and nadis by a trained practitioner. She was wearing a shirt with an image of Archangel Michael on the front, which reminded me of Mont Saint Michele in Normandy, and I could feel his loving energy come through her hands. It was the perfect culmination of my powerful plant medicine experience.

Hippie Village

On the last day of my trip, I had several hours before my flight in the evening, so I spent the afternoon at an extraordinary village on the ocean, which was not far from the airport. It was called *Aldeia Arembepe*, which means *Hippie* in Portuguese, and has been visited by famous rock musicians such as Jimi Hendrix, Janis Joplin, and Mick Jagger.

There was an artisan shopping square, a school, a stage for various performances, a restaurant/bar, and an area for the Brazilian mixed martial arts dance known as *Capoeira*. The unique homes were very inviting, and all the townspeople got together daily to celebrate life through music, sharing food, dancing, and creating art. Everyone seemed to be having a great time, and luckily, two people in my group spoke a bit of Portuguese so I could communicate somewhat with the locals.

People were making jewelry and crafts throughout the village, and there were booths set up with a variety of pieces for sale. I bought a necklace made from the spine of a snake and a unique feather earring from a man whom I discovered had lived in a secluded part of the Amazon for most of his life and had just moved there. I could not imagine living in the jungle after my spider episode and dealing with deadly creatures daily but have much respect and admiration for those who do. I am impressed by the way they survive in harsh conditions with the threat of death always present. You have to be pretty tough to live in the Amazon.

I met a family from France who was sailing around the world on a yacht in search of paradise. They had traveled to many places and planned to settle down once they determined which location was the best one for them. They had heard about Aldeia from a friend and decided to check it out. I was very intrigued by their story, and after speaking with them in both English and the little bit of French I knew, I thought of the following quotes by the French novelist Marcel Proust;

"The real voyage of discovery consists not in seeking new lands but seeing with new eyes"[46]- Marcel Proust
"We don't receive wisdom; we must discover it for ourselves after a journey that no one can take for us or spare us"[47] – Marcel Proust

It reminded me that during all of my travels abroad, I was truly experiencing an inner voyage, enabling me to see with "new eyes..."

As I was leaving the peaceful village, I noticed the frame of a new house overlooking the ocean and imagined what it would be like to build a home in paradise. Then I pondered the idea that paradise is found within and smiled to myself while drinking a beer called *Skol*...

My experiences in Brazil were transformative and paved the way for more travels ahead as I felt both very grounded and ready to soar. I was inspired to express what I had learned through creative outlets and was looking forward to sharing the wisdom with others.

Upon returning home, I started a yoga apparel company and designed logos to represent the concepts and symbols I had embraced throughout my journeys. I created images with the chakras, the Yin Yang, and the mantra for compassion, which touched me so deeply in Brazil - *Om Mani Padme Hum*.

I printed the designs on shirts, shorts, leggings, yoga mat bags, and totes. I sold my line at various yoga studios, stores, and shows and was enjoying my new business venture. It was very gratifying in ways that were beyond the monetary gain, and I was enjoying the positive response from people. It felt great to be in a creative flow in my life once again.

Model - Jessica

Chapter 12
Costa Rica

Soon after launching my yoga apparel business, I decided it was time for another adventure as well as a business trip for my new company. I booked a retreat at a resort in Costa Rica called *Anamaya,* which means "no worries" in Hindi and packed my suitcase with as much of my clothing line as I could fit plus a few outfits to wear. I hadn't been to Costa Rica in quite a while, and as I was sitting in the airport waiting to board my flight, I reflected on an intense spiritual experience I had there one Christmas eve.

Dominical

My ex and I had traveled to Costa Rica many years ago and stayed in a beautiful private home we rented in the middle of the rainforest. When we arrived in the city of San Jose, we rented a small Kia SUV, grabbed a map, and headed on our journey towards a town called Manuel Antonio. The road was unpaved and bumpy the whole way, and we even stopped at a cafe on the side of the road called *The Bumpy Road Café,* and a gentleman informed us that our tire was leaking, most likely due to the rocks we had just driven over for miles. After thanking him for the heads up, we decided to keep driving, as we were told there was a gas station a few miles up the road.

We never made it to the gas station. We got a flat tire along the way, and there was only a small farmhouse in the area, so we sat in the SUV, contemplating what to do next. Neither of us spoke Spanish, and it was a scary prospect walking up to a home in the middle of nowhere to ask for help while unable to communicate. We decided to take our chances and knocked on the door. A friendly man answered who didn't speak any English, so he got one of his relatives to translate for us who contacted the owners of the home we had rented. Luckily, they just happened to be friends with the farmer and told us to wait about an hour for them to arrive and that they would contact the car rental company for us. We were very relieved and grateful for their help.

We discovered that two generations of families from both Costa Rica and Nicaragua were at the farmhouse together for the holidays. The children took me on a tour of the farm, and I fell in love with an adorable pig in a fenced-off area. I noticed one of the men sharpening a large knife in the distance, and as he started walking towards the pen with it, I realized that the pig was actually about to be slaughtered for food. Being an animal lover and vegan, I didn't know what to do and walked quickly towards the front of the house while covering my ears as much as I could to drown out the gut-wrenching, squealing sounds. I couldn't cover them tightly enough and burst into tears until there was silence, and I was both horrified and relieved.

Soon after that awful experience, our hosts arrived at the farmhouse at the same time the rental car company came to repair the tire. They were a wonderful couple who helped us tremendously, and we were glad everything worked out as we followed them back to their home high up in the rainforest about two miles from the main road.
The winding, unpaved narrow road was lined with cliffs, which made for a pretty scary drive even in daylight, and I imagined what it might be like at nightfall.

We arrived at the architecturally stunning home, which had a simple yet elegant decor. The master bedroom upstairs had a shower that was open to the rainforest with Howler monkeys and a variety of other creatures close by in the trees. The entire floorplan was designed to be in harmony with nature. It felt as though the interior was not enclosed but rather a part of the jungle. There was an infinity pool overlooking both the rainforest and the ocean with a full patio, lounge chairs, and a bar stocked with fresh juices and fine wine.

The owner was a German architect, and the entire property was meticulously maintained. His Costa Rican girlfriend was a massage therapist, a Reiki healer, and a chef. They were staying at their beach house about five miles away and said that we could make daily arrangements with them to cook for us in the mornings and evenings using ingredients fresh from their garden and the fruit trees in the area. We thanked them for their hospitality and set up a time for them to make breakfast the following morning.

They came to the house as planned and prepared a spectacular feast, after which we spent the day soaking in the beauty of the rainforest, hiking the nearby trails, and lounging by the pool. It was paradise.

The day before Christmas, we decided to drive a few miles to the closest town called Dominical, which was an international haven for surfers from all parts of the world. We befriended a group of surfers on the beach who were staying in a *lean-to*, which is a simple building with a concrete floor that is open to the elements. It wasn't comfortable, but it only cost them about five dollars per day, and they could surf every day if they so desired. They were all on a tight budget, so we bought them beer and pizza and had a party at their place.

The sun was about to set, and it started to rain, so we decided to head back to our rental. We thought it might be challenging to navigate the roads at night in the heavy rain, so we convinced one of the guys to drive us back up to our place in exchange for staying in one of the guest rooms. He happened to be a Deadhead from the East Coast, and we enticed him to drive us by telling him that we brought a bunch of Grateful Dead CDs with us and had an infinity pool to swim in once we were back at the house. He agreed to take us joking that he was only doing so because of the CDs.

We said goodbye to the surfers and began our ascent up the mountain when it started raining very heavily. The sky just opened up, and the water that poured from it caused major flash flooding on the road. It was pitch black except for our headlights as we took a wrong turn and were unable to figure out which way to go. The rain was coming down so hard that the SUV started sliding backward, and I envisioned a mudslide causing us to drop off the side of the cliff. We all agreed that we needed to get out of the vehicle just in case and I remembered that I had an LED light keychain that I purchased right before the trip with a gut instinct that I would need it for some reason. I realized that my intuition was correct as we trudged through the mud with only my keychain light to guide us.

We were utterly exhausted after about a half-hour of walking uphill but had to keep going regardless. The rain was starting to let up, so we decided to take a break and sit on the wet ground for a bit when all of a sudden, our friend jumped up and screamed that something huge with a bunch of legs had just crawled across his lap. That was all I needed to hear as I bolted straight up and said, "No more stopping." As the three of us continued walking in the direction we were hoping was the right way, the rain started getting heavier once again, and I began to pray.

It was Christmas Eve, and I feared that we might not make it through the dire situation. Although I am not Christian, I found myself calling upon Christ and prayed for him to bring us light to be able to see more than my small LED light keychain could provide and to lead us in the right direction. At that exact moment, we saw two headlights driving up the road towards us, and I couldn't believe my eyes when I realized that it was our hosts. They had forgotten something important at the house that couldn't wait until the morning to retrieve. They asked us what happened and when we told them our story, they remarked that we were lucky that we didn't slide off the cliff with the kind of downpour that had just occurred. They helped us get our SUV out of the mud, and we all went back to the house, turned on some Grateful Dead music, drank some wine, and swam in the infinity pool under the moonlight as the rain subsided.

I am fairly certain that our surfer friend thinks of that night each year as I do, wherever he might be today. It was indeed a Christmas miracle, and the phrase "Jesus Saves" took on a special meaning for me after that experience.

Montezuma

After reflecting on my last trip to Costa Rica while waiting to board the flight, I noticed a young couple doing some yoga stretches. They looked like they were meant for each other, both physically and energetically. Something was very intriguing about them, and I was hoping they would sit next to me on the long flight.

As I boarded the plane and approached my seat, I saw that the couple was in my row... It was interesting that they would be seated next to me on a packed flight with over one hundred people. We began talking, and I discovered that the woman was from Israel, and her husband was from the USA. She reminded me of my friend from Israel, named Sivan, who is like a sister to me. They told me that they were extreme survivalists who enjoyed venturing into dangerous and inhospitable places with basic supplies, a map, and some rations. They planned to take a trip through the rain forest for a week and then attend a friend's wedding in Costa Rica after that. I thought I was a badass until I spoke to them. We had a very spiritual conversation during the flight, which also included a discussion about the concept of synchronicity. When we arrived in Costa Rica, I gave them one of my business cards so we could keep in touch and we went on our separate adventures.

After a two-hour layover and another flight, I finally arrived at the property, which had an infinity pool hanging over the rainforest with the ocean as a backdrop. As I walked through the entrance of the resort, it looked like the set of a bad reality TV show, with vapid Barbie doll types in string bikinis and Ken dolls in surfer shorts. I assumed that they were a part of my group and thought there must be a valuable lesson I needed to learn during the trip. While I was standing by the check-in area, one of the Ken dolls informed me that he and his group were from California and that they were waiting for a shuttle to arrive to take them to the airport. He then proceeded to give me some useful information about the area and was actually quite friendly. At that point, I realized that my lesson was that I shouldn't have been so quick to judge people I didn't know.

After the initial group left, I noticed a very statuesque woman who seemed familiar to me, checking in at the front desk. We started conversing, and I discovered that she thought the same thing about me as we tried to figure out where we might have met, being that she was from Canada, and I was from the USA. She said that she owned a yoga studio, and when she told me the name of it, I must have looked stunned as I replied, "that's the name of my company." At the time, there were only three companies in the world with that same name in Canada, New Zealand, and the USA. What are the chances that two of the three would meet in the middle of the Costa Rican jungle? We bonded instantly and spent the rest of the week learning from one another while having fun. I woke up with the sunrise each morning and did yoga on a wooden platform overlooking the rainforest below while listening to the birds and Howler monkeys. I immersed myself in the sound vibration of the jungle symphony while flowing from one asana (posture) to the next, and it felt incredible.

My small group was awesome. We spent many days together doing yoga, zip-lining through the rainforest, taking day trips to various places, hanging out on the beach, dancing, eating incredible food, drinking wine, and enjoying our time there together.

I asked the owner of the retreat for permission to sell my clothing line if I gave him a percentage of sales to which he agreed, and I sold out in a couple of days. It felt great to have such a positive response to my designs and to see people wearing them.

My experience at Anamaya was fabulous, and I wished that I had some more time to spend there. The day had arrived for our departure, and my group was waiting in the lobby for the airport shuttle. I brought up the subject of spirit animals and described a lesson that I was planning to teach when I returned home on the role of animals in various cultures around the world. I explained that the students are taught about the four categories of totem animals, message, journey, life, and shadow. They are given the task of figuring out at least one totem that resonates with them and then creating a ceramic mug based on their chosen animal. I told them an abbreviated version my owl totem story and said that often when I tell it, owls appear to me in a variety of unusual ways soon after. At that moment, a gentleman was checking in at the front desk, and he was wearing shorts that had owl eyes on the pockets. My group chuckled when they noticed the coincidence, and one of them said, "there's your owl." I laughed and commented that it was likely that more signs would appear.

Our shuttle arrived to take us to the puddle jumper plane and then back to San Jose, where I booked a hotel room for the evening, as I had an early morning flight back home the next day. I didn't realize at the time that I had booked such a fabulous hotel. The décor, food, and drinks were exceptional and I ended up having fun with some people from Florida. It was a great way to spend my last night in Costa Rica.

The next morning as I boarded my flight home, I noticed a Native American man with dark skin, braided black hair, and full sleeve tattoos of famous portraits of Native American tribal chiefs and warriors on both arms. He looked very wise and interesting to me, but I didn't get the opportunity to speak with him as his seat was in the front area of the plane, and mine was in the middle. When I arrived at my row, there was a couple already seated there who was very friendly as I took my aisle seat and we began conversing. I recall thinking that I got lucky again to be next to another great couple on the way home, just like on the flight there. After about an hour of conversation, we began discussing our occupations, and I told them that I was a high school art teacher and a yoga instructor and that I had just attended a retreat in Costa Rica. The woman looked at me quizzically and asked me if my name was Susan, to which I replied, "how do you know my name?" She responded that their good friends sat next to me on the plane over a week ago on the way to Costa Rica... She went on to explain that her friend, the woman from Israel, lost my business card when they went on the survival excursion and was upset because she wanted to touch base with me again in the future. That led to a conversation about synchronicity and other spiritual subjects for the remainder of the flight.

The following events that took place at the end of my journey were so incredible that if I didn't have a picture as proof, it would be really difficult for anyone to believe. As the aircraft landed and the captain made his announcement, his final words were, "On behalf of Frontier Airlines, thank you for flying Ollie the Owl..." I was astounded as I disembarked from the flight, and I couldn't get to the window fast enough to see if there was an owl image on the wing. I knew that Frontier Airlines had animals painted on their planes, but I had never seen one with an owl before. As I approached the window, I was totally blown away...

Feeling as though I was in the same vortex of energy as when I first experienced my owl totem, I caught sight of the Native American man again. We were both on the automatic walkway when I noticed large pictures hanging on the wall of the same Native American chiefs and warriors he had tattooed on his arms. He even looked at the portraits and then back at his tattoos a few times like he recognized the synchronicity as well, but neither of us ever spoke to one another, and we went our separate ways.

I was in such a whirlwind state that I was speechless when my partner Nick came to pick me up in his truck at passenger pick-up. I just calmly explained that I needed a while to process what had just occurred because it was truly unbelievable.

As he started to drive away from the curb, I happened to look to the right and was in total shock when I saw the Ken doll guy from California whom I spoke with at the retreat in Costa Rica before my group arrived...

What were the statistical odds that I had met the man in the middle of the Costa Rican jungle, and he just happened to have been standing on the curb at the airport in Las Vegas right at that moment soon after the other three successive synchronistic occurrences?

He recognized me and waved while quickly asking, "how was your trip?" as we were driving away to which I responded..."EPIC!"

Chapter 13
Deities, Gods & Goddesses

Spiritual Jewelry

I was deeply affected by my experience in Costa Rica and wanted to know more about a variety of spiritual beliefs around the world. I felt inspired to design jewelry again after taking a break for a while and I created pieces representing certain deities, the chakras, and other spiritual symbols. I sold my jewelry along with my clothing line at yoga studios, events, and festivals. My partner Nick and I set up elaborate sales booths, which was both a lot of work and a lot of fun. He was instrumental in starting my company and helping me in many ways along the way. He is patient, meticulous, and an incredible problem-solver. I could not have done it without him.

I enjoyed speaking with people about the symbolism, techniques, and intentions of my creations and helping them find the right piece for each of them. It was gratifying to help them in some small way as they shared personal struggles with me. The jewelry seemed to help them feel better when they tried it on, which sometimes resulted in some profound spiritual interactions.

I created gemstone Mala Beads used for meditation and incorporated a variety of concepts and deity symbols into the designs along with accompanying mantras to invoke compassion, healing, protection, and abundance. Malas contain 108 beads and are usually made from wood, gemstones, seeds, and other materials strung together with a *Guru* (teacher) bead at the head to represent all great teachers and sages.

I facilitated Mala Meditation workshops at my friend Angelica's studio for yoga teachers in training and designed custom Mala Beads for many of the participants. I met with them individually, and we discussed both their desires and challenges while choosing particular gemstones to resonate with each person. I used the chakra system as a guide for them to understand why they were experiencing some of the issues that were deterring them from achieving their goals and dreams. I received wonderful feedback from the women, which inspired me to create unique gemstone bracelets as well.

While I was set up at a local studio, I became friends with one of the employees in charge of merchandise named Cristina. She also created a clothing line, so we decided to split a booth at a yoga event called *Shaktifest,* which takes place in Joshua Tree, California, each year. There was a tarot card reader named Nikki in an area next to us who did a reading for me. The card she pulled said, "Your life purpose involves writing, reading, editing, or selling spiritually based books. Archangel Gabriel is the *messenger angel* who helps writers, teachers, and others involved in delivering spiritual messages."

In a state of bewilderment, I told her what the *Council of Elders* had said about me writing a book. I also mentioned my channeling experience with *Gabriel* and the owl. After discussing my reluctance to write in the past because I didn't know where to begin, she assured me that it was inevitable that I would write a book and that *Gabriel* would be a source of inspiration and guidance for me along the way.

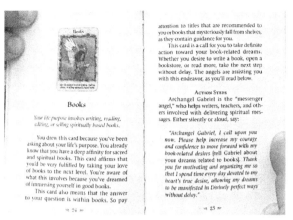

Figure 23

When I returned to the booth and told Cristina about my reading, she was very intrigued by the message as well. Little did we know at the time that the following synchronicity would happen a few years later...

Cristina and I met for drinks recently, and I told her that I was finally writing a book about synchronicity, just as my tarot card reading had predicted. As luck would have it, she had decided to design book covers with her unique style of art and said that she would love to create mine to which I responded, "absolutely." She emailed the cover to me a week later, and I was thrilled with the result, as it truly captured the essence of my story.[48]

Inspiration works in mysterious ways. While writing this chapter, I got the idea to create a jewelry line based on the concepts and symbols presented in the book (www.owlsage.com).

The Hindu Gods and Goddesses

In the Hindu pantheon of gods and goddesses, I have felt connected to a group of five particular deities who embody certain qualities and attributes. I immersed myself in learning about them and working with their energies by chanting their mantras and displaying statues of them around my home. They have had a significant impact on my spiritual growth, and I have mentioned a few of them in earlier chapters. They are multilayered in meaning, which is expressed through the images and symbols that are associated with each deity. It is the underlying energy behind the visual imagery which one can harness to achieve a desired outcome. In doing so, however, it is important to understand that these deities are very powerful and must be approached with the utmost respect and gratitude.

Shiva - (part of the trinity of Brahma the cosmic egg and Vishnu the Preserver)
Creator, Preserver, and Protector, Destroyer, and Transformer- aides in overcoming one's ego for optimal spiritual growth
Ganesha - (the elephant deity and son of Shiva)
Remover of Obstacles, Bestower of Wisdom, Challenger- aides in overcoming obstacles and creates challenges to acquire wisdom
Kali - (the female counterpart of Shiva)
Destroyer of Evil and Ego, Protector, Bestower of Moksha (liberation, passion, and bliss)- aides in protection from evil and overcoming the ego to achieve Moksha
Saraswati - (the female counterpart of Vishnu)
Goddess of Music, Art, Literature, Nature, and Wisdom - aides in acquiring wisdom through all creative pursuits
Lakshmi - (the sister of Saraswati and consort of Vishnu) - Goddess of Prosperity, Abundance, Wealth and Good Fortune - aides in manifesting all forms of abundance and gratitude (connected to owls and elephants)

Shiva   Ganesha   Kali   Saraswati   Lakshmi

There is a graceful yoga pose called *Natarajasana* (King Dancer) representing Shiva in the dance of the cosmos, and I have practiced it in a variety of places around the world. Shiva Nataraja always reminds me to dance joyfully through life, no matter what challenges I may face, while keeping my balance and strength intact.

Ganesha is Shiva's son in Hindu mythology. He has been a vital part of my life and has helped me overcome obstacles, such as during the sweat lodge ceremony in Brazil. I have often felt protected and encouraged by his commanding presence to move out of my comfort zone in search of new experiences, which has challenged me to grow.

All three goddesses, *Kālī, Lakshmi,* and *Saraswati,* represent various aspects of the main goddess, who is often referred to as *Devi, Durga,* or *Lalita.* They each embody the feminine principle of *Shakti,* which is the energy of all of creation.

Kālī, who is the Hindu goddess of fire, appears like a roaring flame. She is a fierce protector and is often pictured with a blue face and a long, pointy, protruding tongue. She has many arms holding weapons to fight evil, wears a garland of skulls, and is stepping on Shiva to represent the dissolution of the ego. Her energy is very tumultuous at first, like setting a log on fire and adding an accelerant. After a while, she smolders as burning ash until it is time to add more fuel again. When I am feeling a bit stuck creatively, and in need of inspiration, she challenges me to ignite my inner flame of passion, then aides me on my quest for experiences that break down my ego, while teaching me valuable life lessons. She is a force to be reckoned with and not to be taken lightly.

One evening after calling upon Kali for guidance and inspiration, I was at a party where there was a bonfire within a pit shaped like a boat. A guest handed me a small firecracker to throw into the fire with a faded image on the front that looked like Kali. He suggested I release everything negative while throwing it into the flames. I happened to be wearing a Kali bracelet that I had made at the time and welcomed the synchronicity as I tossed the firecracker into the fire and released some things. It felt very cathartic, and I experienced a significant shift in my energy that night.

The following day, my good friend Gina and I went hiking in the Desert. As we walked throughout the red rock pillar formations, ironically named *The Valley of Fire*, Kali's presence came in so powerfully that I had to sit and cool down for a bit. I gazed at the beautiful rocks that resembled flames in front of me while I focused on the things that required attention in my life. I could feel Kali's fierce but protective nature as I went through some much-needed self-reflection. It was an intense experience that is difficult to describe, but I felt renewed and empowered to move forward with making some important decisions.

Gina and I went to see a Led Zeppelin cover band concert that evening, and as we were walking past the box office window, she pointed to an image of Kali on the front of it... I walked up to the painting reproduction and noticed that the artist's name was *Athena*, which was another sign for me, as she is a Greek godess I connect with who is often pictured with an owl to represent wisdom. I had a feeling that we were about to have a great time as we entered the concert venue. The hypnotic songs put me in a trance as I moved to the rhythm like I was dancing inside of the music. It was an extraordinary night, and I was thankful for Kali's fierce, protective, and passionate presence in my life once again.

Lakshmi comes forth at various times bringing abundance in the form of material and spiritual wealth. She has brought me both, and I am truly grateful for all that I have received. Like the Greek goddess Athena, she is portrayed at times with an owl to represent the wisdom of manifesting desires and appreciating the gifts.

Lakshmi appeared to me when I was selling my jewelry at a wholesale merchandise show, which was the first one I had ever participated in since starting my company. I arrived at the convention center and began silently chanting a Lakshmi mantra before setting up my space.

Through what I felt was divine intervention, the people in the booth next to me backed out of the show for some reason, and I was able to extend my five-foot space to ten-feet with no extra charge. I set up my jewelry with unique displays and received quite a bit of attention and sales.

There were some very nice gentlemen from Nepal in a booth across from me selling mini statues of Hindu deities. They didn't have a bank card reader, and they were being charged a lot more interest by entering the sales manually, so I gave them my extra one to use during the show. They thanked me profusely, and then one of them came up to my booth a few minutes later and handed me a statue of Lakshmi to bring me good fortune.

Soon after receiving the statue, a buyer walked up and placed a substantial order for her store. She also happened to be a Grateful Dead fan as well, and we discussed the likelihood of being at many of the same concerts over the years. The rest of the show was a great success, and I felt convinced that reciting mantras can be very effective.

Saraswati's graceful presence comes in softly as she inspires my creativity and enjoyment of literature, music, and the arts. She appears whenever I am about to embark on a journey, new endeavor, or creative project.

Around the time that I was struggling with the first few sentences of my book, I pulled the *Saraswati* card from my Goddess Oracle deck along with the *Cube* card from my Sacred Geometry deck. I felt that they were both inspirational messages for me to remove doubt and begin writing, which I did soon after.

I am so grateful to have been led to discover the Hindu deities, gods, and goddesses and work with their energies. I believe that they are happy to bestow their protection, gifts, and wisdom when they are called upon by an individual or group doing so with positive intentions, respect, and gratitude.

Chapter 14
Indonesia

Bali

As I was delving more in depth into both Buddhism and Hinduism, I chose another journey abroad to a country that has a unique blend of both belief systems. The timing was perfect as my good friend Jada and her husband Alvin decided to host a yoga retreat in Bali, Indonesia, through the studio they owned at the time. Bali is a yoga retreat paradise with many diverse and sacred places to visit. Indonesia was at the top of my travel destination list, so when she mentioned that the studio was hosting the retreat there, I told her to include me.

Another reason I wanted to travel to Indonesia was to visit a sacred temple called *Borobudur,* which is a 9th-century Mahayana Buddhist structure in Central Java. It is the world's largest Buddhist temple and consists of nine stacked platforms, which are in a pyramid shape as a three-dimensional Sri Yantra symbol. I decided to book a day trip in advance to the small city of Yogyakarta and was thrilled that there was also a Hindu temple dedicated to Lord Shiva called *Prambanan* that was part of the tour. When I told the two women who were going to be my roommates in Bali about it, they also decided to book it in advance.

My flight to Indonesia had connections with very long layovers in both California and Australia, so it took me almost two days to finally arrive at the resort in the middle of the evening. I had trouble falling asleep on the uncomfortable flights, and I was totally exhausted and looking forward to finally having a bed to sleep in once I made it there. Even though it was dark, I could tell that the place was magnificent.

The retreat was called *Desa Seni*, which is the place I mentioned where the quote cards were placed on my bed during the turndown service. The yoga sessions were invigorating, and the service and attention to detail were both outstanding. The cuisine was made with fresh ingredients from the gardens on the property and was presented beautifully. My cottage was perfect, and the saltwater pool was very refreshing after the many rigorous daily activities.

One evening, we had a local Balinese dance group perform a sacred dance that was captivating. Throughout the performance, the women moved their hands hypnotically in unison as their eyes looked repeatedly left to right. It is said that they shift their eyes back and forth so they can be aware of all things, including danger and evil. I took a photo and was awed by the presence of a giant orb resembling the moon above the musicians, with smaller ones around the dancers.

We visited an ancient monkey natural habitat, sacred temples, Balinese theatres, beaches, markets, and an incredible outdoor sculpture park with giant sculptures of Hindu deities, particularly Vishnu, the preserver, and his sacred steed, Garuda.

The people give daily offerings called *Canang Sari*, which loosely translates to the "essence of a basket of flowers." They are usually small square or floral-shaped boxes made of palm or banana leaves, which are filled with fresh flowers, money, a tiny bit of food, and a burning incense stick placed on top. New offerings are set out every day in most temples, homes, and throughout the streets of Bali. The ancient ritual has special significance as an act of honoring the deities and showing gratitude for all aspects of life. They are not to be walked over when they are on the ground nor moved until it is time to do so. It is crucial to know a country's sacred customs in order not to violate them and offend the people.

The cultural beliefs and practices of the Balinese people are both traditional and meaningful in a way that truly embodies a spiritual connection to nature, and the cycles of life. It was refreshing waking up every morning and seeing the beautiful *Canang Saris* everywhere.

During one of the outings, my group went to a local woodworking artisan market. There were superbly crafted wooden statues of the deities all over the place, and I was on sensory overload the entire time. An artist was working on a beautiful statue of the goddess Saraswati, and when I inquired about it, he told me that he had just finished a similar one and brought me inside the shop to show it to me.

I held the delicate and exquisitely carved statue in my hands and said immediately, "I'll take her." Then I spotted a statue of Ganesha that I felt drawn to, so I purchased them both. I was concerned at first about how I would pack them into my small luggage but knew that I would figure it out somehow.

Borobudur and Prambanan

The following day, my roommates and I took a two-hour flight from the retreat to *Yogyakarta* and the temple *Borobudur* that I was so excited to see. When we arrived there, our guide met us at the airport, and we set out on our journey. We visited a magnificent royal palace where the Sultan resided, a famous *Batik* (decorative fabric) and silver jewelry store, and then had lunch at a great Ganesha themed cafe. The people in Java were friendly, and our guide was fantastic as she brought us from one destination to the next. When we arrived at

Borobudur, I felt the same excitement that I did while visiting Mont Saint Michele in Normandy and Machu Picchu in Peru. I couldn't wait to circle the temple, which was built on a mound with no known interior structure. There were over 500 Buddha statues spread throughout the site, and the walls of the pyramid were covered in over 2,500 square meters of exquisite relief carvings depicting the life and teachings of Buddha. I imagined how many people must have worked for many years to create such a masterpiece of construction, along with the relief carvings and *stupas* (shrines), to pay tribute to Buddha.

As our temple guide took us around the complex, he gave us some great information about the history and explained what some of the relief carvings symbolized. I noticed that a type of tree was prevalent throughout the stories, and I asked our guide about it. He said that it was a sacred *Kalpataru* tree, which means "wish-granting tree" in Sanskrit, so I touched the relief carving and made a wish.

When we arrived at the apex of the temple overlooking the spectacular lush greenery, mountains, and volcanoes, we were instructed to walk three times around the many Buddha *stupas* arranged in a circle while saying prayers and giving thanks. A *stupa* is a dome-shaped shrine symbolizing the universe and is a place of worship and prayer.

Our guide told us that there was one special Buddha stupa, which people from all over the world make offerings to in exchange for their wishes to be granted. When I asked why that particular one was so special, he informed us that there were bombs planted in a few of them by terrorists years ago, and the one in the lucky Buddha did not detonate like the others. I made an offering by placing a piece of jewelry I had made with an Aum symbol on it inside the stupa as I made my wish.

Borobudur was exquisite, and I felt blessed to have been able to draw a line through it on my temple bucket list.

Our next stop was *Prambanan,* which was a complex of temples with statues throughout the site that was built during the 9th century to honor the trinity of Hindu gods. There were eight main temples and eight smaller shrines within the central compound. The three largest temples were dedicated to the *Trimurti* (three Hindu gods) - *Brahma* (cosmic egg), *Vishnu* (preserver), and Shiva (transformer). Shiva's temple is the largest and centrally located as a focal point. When Prambanan was constructed, it was dedicated to Shiva and bore the name *Shivagrha,* which means "House of *Shiva.*"

The complex contains the ruins of over two hundred smaller temples, and I could only imagine how magnificent it must have looked when it was first built. I found an actual Kalpataru tree and posed for a photo in Vriksasana (tree pose) beneath it while making another wish.

We left Prambanan as the sun was setting on the horizon and thanked our guide for such a fabulous day as she drove us back to the airport. On the flight back to Bali, I thought about the fact that I had just explored two of the most incredible ancient temples embodying both Buddhism and Hinduism, and I was overcome with gratitude for the experience.

A couple of days later, I visited a Balinese temple on the ocean called *Tanah Lot* with a few people from the retreat. It was constructed around the 16th century to honor the spirits of the sea, and according to Balinese mythology, a Brahmin Priest named *Niratha* had it built high atop the rock formation because it resembled a ship on the ocean. However, he had to fight a giant sea serpent to be able to build the temple there, as the rock was his domain. When Niratha won the battle, he allowed the serpent to stay at the temple as long as he agreed to be a guardian against evil. It is believed that the serpent still protects the temple to this day.

On the walkway to the beach below, a Balinese man was holding a giant snake around his neck. He was taking photos of tourists with the snake, so I posed for a photo and bought it. I was with a woman from my group who was deathly afraid of snakes, and she couldn't believe I had just taken a picture with it wrapped around my neck.

I quickly explained the concept of the shadow totem and my life-changing encounter with the spider in Brazil so that she might be inspired to face her fear and take a picture too. I was impressed when she did. It was a courageous and transformative moment for her, and I sensed a shift in her energy soon after that was quite profound.

We walked along the beach to a cave, which was said to be the home of many holy snakes. There was a man dressed in white who blessed us at the entrance and guided us to a snake nestled inside a crevice. It is believed that if you drink from the flowing water at the mouth of the cave, and then touch the snake, you will be protected and rewarded in life. Of course, I did both, and to my amazement, so did my friend.

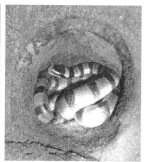

Before leaving *Tanah Lot*, we walked to a small shrine across from the temple overlooking the sea, and I chanted a mantra of gratitude called the *Gayatri* mantra, which invokes the light and dispels the darkness. It was a powerful moment for us both.

On the way back to the retreat, I spotted my friend Jada all alone on the side of the road, looking completely distraught and stressed out. Our driver pulled up to her in the car, and she looked both shocked and relieved to see us. We were about five miles from the property at that point as she explained that she had gone out with a group for a bike ride and then got separated and lost. She was frantically trying to get directions, but people didn't understand her and kept giving her the wrong information. After explaining to us what had happened, she picked up her bike and somehow fit it into the tour guide's car. He was great about it, which helped calm her down. When we returned to the retreat, Jada was happy to be lounging by the pool with a glass of wine in her hand, safe and sound. We discussed the synchronicity between us yet again, as I just happened to be passing by her at that moment. Although we didn't have an explanation, we both understood that for some unknown reason, we are connected.

The following morning, I wrenched my back getting out of my bed when my foot got twisted in the mosquito net, and I was forced to take it easy for the last two days before the long flight home. I had to pack my suitcase the night before my flight and was not able to fit the statues that I had purchased at the artisan's market. I wrapped them both in newsprint and put Saraswati in a shopping bag and Ganesha in my backpack.

On the morning of my departure, I relaxed on a chaise by the pool with one of the local dogs that I bonded with, trying to muster up the strength it would take to endure the long and likely painful journey ahead. I wore my turquoise Ganesha hoodie to call upon his help with the challenges that I would face. When my shuttle arrived to take me to the airport, I put my backpack on and began walking towards the lobby. I expected to be in pain as I took each step, but to my total surprise, I was fine while I had it on. The Ganesha statue was carved from a section of a tree that was cut in half, creating a flat back. It was positioned perfectly on my lower lumbar inside the backpack, and it somehow alleviated the pain due to the weight and placement of it. Ganesha, the remover of obstacles, literally had my back...

As I waited on the long line during the boarding process, I spoke with a mother and daughter from Australia who had just spent time at a yoga retreat in another part of Bali. I enjoyed our conversation, and as we walked down the aisle to find our seats, it turned out that they were seated in my row... I remarked about the synchronicity, which led to a discussion about spirituality. The mother told me that she had just learned about the chakras and wanted to know more about them. I just happened to have a DVD with me about the chakras, which I let her borrow to watch during the flight. She thanked me as she plugged her headphones into the DVD player while I attempted to get comfortable.

I devised a way to alleviate the pain in my back by positioning my backpack on the seat behind my lower spine. When I needed to use the bathroom, I just slipped it on, and I was fine. After a seven-hour flight, I landed in Australia for a long layover before heading back to America, and I was able to walk without pain the whole time thanks to my statue.

I finally made it back to the USA, and Nick picked me up at the airport once again after another great journey. I was so happy to see him and couldn't wait to show him my pictures with my narration, of course. As we pulled up to the house, I thanked Ganesha for helping me get there as I thought to myself, "no matter where I may roam, I am always grateful for my home..."

"Not all those who wander are lost."[49]- JRR Tolkien

Reflections

My experiences at the yoga retreats that I have visited over the past ten years have contributed tremendously to my life and spiritual growth. If I had not discovered yoga, I would be a different person. I have made many choices without fearing possible obstacles, which has enabled me to venture out into the unknown and come back to the comforts of my life at home with great stories to share.

As a result of my travels, I have acquired much knowledge and have become a better teacher. I have a broader perspective of the diverse cultures around the world through their art, beliefs, customs, history, and architecture, which I can bring to life in my classroom with examples, pictures, and stories. Through my experiences and the wisdom that I have gained, I am able to inspire others to want to learn and grow, even if they don't have the ability or means to travel. The inner journey can be inspired by books, videos, music, theatre, yoga, mind medicine, and meditation without venturing abroad.

We are all on different paths in life, and it is up to an individual to decide which one to walk. The one that I have chosen works for me, and it may not work for someone else.

I believe that every person has a story to tell, and the struggles that we must sometimes endure can often be a catalyst for growth, just as the lotus seed blossoms from the mud into a beautiful and resilient flower resting above the water.

We have the free will to create meaning in our lives, regardless of our circumstances, and can manifest what we need through positive intentions and a willingness to be open to the lessons that we learn along the way. Life is a voyage into the unknown depths of limitless possibilities and is navigated in every moment with each breath.

As human beings, we have been given the unique capacity to contemplate our existence and co-create our lives. When we discover what we are most passionate about, we can move in the direction of manifesting the things we desire by making conscious choices. If we cultivate a clear vision of what we wish to accomplish or obtain, the energy imprint is set in motion, and the way is shown.

People who are successful and happy have mastered the ability to recognize opportunities, which can often be synchronistic signs that show up at the perfect time to lead a person in a direction that determines his/her destiny. The key is to pay attention and be open to the messages being conveyed.

It is through insight, intuition, choice, and action that we can decide to paint a masterpiece rather than languish in front of a blank canvas. There are always pivotal choices we make, for better or worse. The life we create is inexorably linked to our karma, so it is important to have integrity with our intentions.

Part Five

Integrity and Intention

Positive Thoughts & Actions

Manifest Favorable Outcomes

Chapter 15
Portugal and Portal Days

Integrity, Intention and The Mayan Calendar

I feel that both integrity and intention are the cornerstones of creating a meaningful life, and I decided to teach my students a lesson on the subject by incorporating the concepts into a poster project. As I was looking for paper to write down some ideas, I just happened to find a small book called *The Intender's Handbook* by Tony Burroughs, which I hadn't seen in years... I planned to introduce the assignment by discussing the meaning of the word integrity, which is one of our school's values. I directed the students to set an intention with integrity for their lives by inspiring them with the following quote; "Watch your thoughts, for they become your words; watch your words, for they become your actions; watch your actions, for they become your habits; watch your habits, for they become your character; watch your character, for it becomes your destiny."– Lao Tsu

A few days after writing my lesson plan, I noticed that the quote was hanging on the bulletin board across from my classroom... I hadn't mentioned my idea to anyone and felt it was a sign.

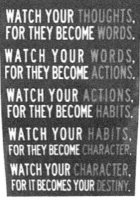

Today is 1st of the 2nd 10 portal days in a row in the Mayan calendar. So I just wanted you to be aware for next 9 days that time is expanded..And you can manifest things much faster if you visualize the idea or project.. I thought you would want to know.. love & miss you xoxo Michelle

Figure 24

The morning before teaching the project, my friend Michelle texted me before school to inform me that the next nine days were going to be portal days, according to the Mayan Calendar. Michelle is very informed about the wisdom known as the *Law of Time*, which is

172

considered to be the natural flow of time and measurement. There is an organization called *The Foundation of The Law of Time* that outlines a 13 moon (month) calendar year that is based on the *Mayan Toltec* model. It utilizes a ratio of 13:20, which is a natural timing frequency as coded in the 13 x 20 unit *Tzolkin*.

The Gregorian calendar is based on a ratio of 12:60, which is an artificial timing frequency with an irregular 12-month calendar and a mechanical 60-minute hour. It is believed that the effect of this time construct is contributing to some of the issues in modern civilization, resulting in what is known as the *Technosphere*, which operates at the expense of the biosphere by wasting and not replenishing natural resources at an alarming rate.

Furthermore, many people are feeling disconnected from nature and the creative process, which affects us collectively as a species. It seems that the human race is in a rush against time in the pursuit of material wealth and out of synch with the universal, creative, natural order.

In the Tzolkin Mayan Calendar, there are 260 days, with 52 of the days considered portal days of amplified energy. According to the calendar, there is a layout of the days that are grouped together at various times during the year. The pattern that emerges from it is in the configuration of two mirror-image pyramids linked at the center, which creates a Sri Yantra. This indicates yet another symbolic reference to universal consciousness. It is believed there is a connection between the portal days, the moon cycles, and our DNA, which is why the power of manifestation is magnified. The occurrence of synchronicity happens more frequently during portal days as well.

The *Noosphere* is described as the earth's mind-sphere and is considered to be the mental sheath around the planet. The concept and term were jointly coined in 1926 by Édouard Le Roy, a French philosopher, Pierre Teilhard de Chardin, a Jesuit paleontologist, and Vladimir Vernadsky, a Russian geochemist in Paris.

It is said that the biosphere is linked to the *Noosphere*, creating a unified field of energy. Through our intentions, we can manifest great things for ourselves and humanity by projecting our desires on to the *Noosphere*, especially during portal days.

The information about the Mayan Calendar and the true nature of time was brought forth by a man named Jose Arguelles/Valum Votan who channeled the information in order to bring a natural balance back to our planet. *The Foundation of the Law of Time* was created to relay it to the masses, and they have many books available on their website www.*lawoftime.org*. Their creativity motto is, "Time is Art,"[50]

After receiving Michelle's text in the early morning, I began teaching the concept by asking the students for examples of integrity and setting an intention. They brainstormed some different possibilities for a word that would best express the meaning of both and wrote them down on paper. As I collected the words from the students, I saw that one of them had chosen the word *Noosphere*... She had no idea about the *Law of Time* or the Mayan Calendar and said she was just looking up cool words for the project on her cell phone. We were amazed by the synchronicity when we also realized that I had given her the book *The Celestine Prophecy* to read, just as I had done with my former student Erica.

The following school year, I decided to adjust the lesson to include self-reflection, and I needed my glasses to be able to view my laptop, so I opened a cabinet drawer to look for them. I came across one of Deepak Chopra's books titled, *Synchrodestiny*, and a square piece of reflective mirror cardstock fell out and onto the floor. It was a sample of one of the products that I had ordered for my students to use in a future project someday, and I must have put it in there as a bookmark.

The book is about "Harnessing the infinite power of coincidence to create miracles," as is stated on the front cover. I decided to open it to a random page, and the subject Deepak was discussing just happened to be intention... "Intent works by harnessing the creative forces inherent in the universe. Just as we have our own personal creativity, the universe also displays creativity."[51]- Deepak Chopra.

It was yet another synchronistic experience with one of Deepak's books. I felt that it was a sign that the mirror should be incorporated into the poster to express self-reflection, and it could be cut into a particular shape to represent their intentions. One student created a design which states, "You become and attract what you think." She cut the mirror into a heart and put a *Starry Night* mask over the eyes.

Figure 25

The Organ and the Judge

The last time Michelle had texted me about Portal Days was right before a trip to Portugal, which was planned to celebrate my birthday and my niece's graduation from high school. I had spent many months working out all the details for an eight-day journey starting in Porto, which is in Northern Portugal and working our way down the coast to the Algarve region in the South. I had done much research and chose a variety of places to stay and visit.

I flew to New York a few days before our flight to Portugal to visit my parents. They have been married for over fifty-five years and still love each other deeply. My mother is a very generous and caring person who enjoys life to the fullest between all of her fun activities and spending time with her family. She is also a force to be reckoned with and doesn't let anyone take advantage of her or the people she loves.

My father, who is still a total badass, was a police Sargent for many years until he became a real estate broker in New York after retiring from the police force. They both currently run the real estate office that my father started over fifty years ago. I am very fortunate to have such supportive, loving parents and appreciate everything they have done for me throughout my life.

My father has had many synchronistic experiences in his life as well and was excited that I was planning to write a book about it. He told me a story about the time he had purchased the top of an antique 1865 Estey Pump Organ in Maine that he intended to use as a decorative shelf. It was in my parents' basement for over ten years, and my father happened to be reading an antique reference collector's book and saw the complete organ, so he made a mental note of it.

Two years later, he saw an advertisement for an Estey Pump Organ for sale. It was valued at $3,500 in the collector's book, but the owner was asking only $350, so he decided to check it out. He went to the owner's house to see it and found that it was in excellent condition except for the fact that it was missing the top piece. He bought the organ, transported it to his home, and retrieved the top that he had purchased many years ago from the basement. When he placed it on the organ, he was utterly astounded because it fit perfectly, right down to the missing and broken dowels in both pieces. It was incredible that the organ and the top found each other after possibly being separated for over a century.

Another experience my father had with synchronicity was when he was a police officer, and he brought a defendant before a judge. When the judge delivered his sentencing, he said to the defendant, who had committed grand larceny and three counts of leaving the scene of an auto accident, "I hereby banish you from Nassau County, New York." My father was amused by the judge's unorthodox sentencing, as it reminded him of the no-nonsense way things were handled in the distant past.

Over forty years later, my father was at a retired police officer's breakfast when the conversation turned to the memory of the judge and his use of the word "banishment." After breakfast, he visited an antique shop, and as he walked through the entrance, sitting on a table in the front of the store, was the judge's nameplate, a gavel, a desk piece with pens and badges, a judicial certificate, and a law degree. He was so astounded by the synchronicity and felt that he was destined to have the judge's memorabilia, so he purchased the items, placed them on display in his office, and sometimes uses the gavel at meetings.

One day a man entered his office needing a short-term rental and noticed the judge's nameplate on display. He asked my father if he knew the judge, and my dad responded that he did, at which point the man said the word "banishment." He had been friends with the judge for many years and told my dad that it was his favorite word.

I had a fascinating synchronistic experience with my father right before his eightieth birthday. We were talking about spirit animals, and I told him about the time I had looked in the mirror and saw my owl totem. He remarked that he had just seen a Native American mirror that was left behind in the basement of a house his office was listing, and he thought I might be interested in it.

I asked him to take a picture of it with his cell phone and send it to me, which he did a few hours later, while informing me that it wasn't what he had initially thought it was. He had seen it in the dark and assumed it was a mirror, but it was actually a fabric wall hanging of a Native American chief with feathers all around it.

As I looked at the picture, I was amazed at the resemblance of my dad to the chief... I told him that I thought it was indeed a mirror and that he saw himself in the image. We both wondered if it was a sign of one of my dad's past lives as an Indian chief. I have always felt a strong connection to the Native American culture, so we discussed the possibility that I may have had a past life as a Native American Indian. too. Once again, it was all very fascinating to speculate.

The Black Cube

The day before we left for Portugal, my family and I went shopping at *The Sunrise Mall* in my hometown. It used to be my old hang out when I was growing up, and I hadn't been there in over thirty years. Back then, there was a giant sculpture of a black cube, balancing on one of its' points, that was displayed in the parking lot of the mall where we all used to meet up before cell phones were invented. It was no longer there, and my sister and I reminisced about the fact that we used to wait in line for Grateful Dead tickets next to the cube at the ticket sales booth back in the day. I am mentioning this cube because it will make an appearance later.

Majestic Porto

The following morning, we boarded our flight to Portugal and excitedly headed out to the adventure awaiting us. We arrived in Lisbon and met the driver I had arranged to take us on a three-hour car ride up the coast to the picturesque and vibrant city of Porto.

Our stay there was wonderful, and our hotel was perfectly located alongside the river and street, which was bustling with music, art, and colorful people below our balconies. We visited famous port wineries, took a boat tour along the river, a private car tour of some historic landmarks, ate great food, shopped, and enjoyed the cafes at night.

One morning we had brunch at a beautiful resort called *The Yeatman*, which overlooks the river with great city views. The lobby had a sweeping staircase in the center with a glass ceiling above it, which illuminated the interior of the hotel. We were served a fabulous vegan meal created by a five-star Michelin Chef along with port wine from the region and it was a truly memorable culinary experience.

Later that day, while shopping in the central part of the city, we came across a cafe with a long line out front called, *The Majestic Café*, which just happened to be the place where J.K. Rowling began writing *Harry Potter,* so we waited on the line and were seated soon after.

As I sat in the cafe, I realized the synchronicity of being there while ideas for my book were brewing in my thoughts. I envisioned her seated at one of the tables deep in the throes of writing. I wondered if I would be able to start writing one day and if the words would flow as they did for her. I also thought about the fact that the owl is a part of the Harry Potter series representing magic, wisdom, and protection, and that I was planning to write about my owl totem.[52]

After the Majestic Cafe, while enjoying the sites of Porto, we came across a giant black cube balancing on one point with a bird on top...

My sister and I looked at each other and exclaimed, "there it is... the black cube from the Sunrise Mall!" We felt like we were in an episode of The Twilight Zone and decided to go back there to have dinner that evening at a great restaurant next to the cube. As we were sitting at our table, a black cat appeared, and I thought it might be a sign as the black cat totem seemed to be coming up quite a bit for me at that time. It turned out to be significant several months later.

We enjoyed our time in Porto immensely and spent our last night there watching a local band at one of the cafes, after which we went back to the hotel to sleep as we had to wake up early in the morning to meet our driver.

Mystical Sintra

Our next destination was a mystical town called Sintra, located by the coast in between Porto and Lisbon, which is the main city of Portugal. We arrived there in the morning before check-in so we could leave our luggage at our hotel called *Chateau Saudade*, which was a beautiful Victorian building that had many symbolic objects throughout the hallways and the lobby area. The front gate had a design of two trees on it, one with leaves and one without, and the entrance of the hotel had a flight of ceramic birds alongside the window to the right. My sister Kim noticed the birds first and remarked, "What's with all the birds we keep seeing everywhere?" I realized as soon as she said that, it was a sign for me as I thought back to the beginning of the summer.

I was at a graduation party at the end of the school year and had an interesting conversation with a friend of mine. He and I have had many philosophical discussions, and although he claimed to be an atheist, he would surprise me by saying some pretty profound things, which inspired me in many ways. He professed that the key to enjoying life to the fullest is by allowing all experiences to come and go without attachment, as they are fleeting. While he was speaking, I envisioned a flight of birds as I thought once again about Carpe Diem and the freedom of living in the moment. I thanked him for his insight and realized that in his own way, he was talking about the Buddhist principle of detachment.

Once the summer officially began, I sat in my Zen backyard almost every morning and meditated. I designed a labyrinth using white beach sand and rocks to delineate the pathway both inward and outward. A labyrinth is a maze that enables one to walk while focusing on manifesting desires and releasing stagnant energy and negativity. They have been used for centuries all over the world, and the one I created was a traditional seven-circuit configuration in the shape of a brain.

Walking a labyrinth helps to balance both sides of the body and mind as you move to the center and back out again, while inspiring deep introspection. I meditated in my labyrinth almost every morning at sunrise and then relaxed on my chaise, coffee in hand, while watching the birds flying overhead.

At a certain time each day, hummingbirds would appear all around to drink from the flowering plants, and it reminded me of my time in Brazil. Interestingly, around sundown each day, three tiny bats would fly over the labyrinth in a figure eight back and forth repeatedly like they were drawn to the energy there. Bats are a symbol of mystery and transformation, and I had a feeling that my trip to Portugal was about to teach me a great deal.

I decided to do some shopping a few weeks before the trip and just happened to find a shirt that had a flock of birds on the back along the spine with the words "Be wild and free" on the front pocket. It was symbolic of my vision and morning meditations, so I bought it and packed it in my suitcase to take with me.

When my sister commented on all the birds we kept seeing I recalled my conversation with my friend and realized the synchronicity.

The Initiation Well

I had booked a tour for the afternoon in Sintra at a historical site called *Quinta da Regaleira*, which is a mysterious place with an eclectic mix of Egyptian, Greek, Gothic, Renaissance, and Moorish features. It sits high up on a hill between a medieval Moorish castle at the top, and a Romanticist Palace called *Pena Palace* below.

One of the features that interested me on the grounds of the estate was a spiral stairwell called *Poço Iniciático,* which translates to "Initiation Well." It was designed as a transformative structure promoting self-reflection, growth, and change. After learning about the history and symbolism, I was looking forward to experiencing it.

Sintra has a microclimate, and it was a cloudy, misty day as we made our way up the long, winding road. It felt as though we were in a time warp between the castle, palace, and rock wall structures along the way. The trees were extraordinary, and the scene was surreal, like we were in some mystical land during the reign of King Arthur.

We were running late due to traffic, and we didn't make it in time for the tour, which turned out to be a blessing in disguise as we were able to wander around the property at our own pace while listening to an information wand.

 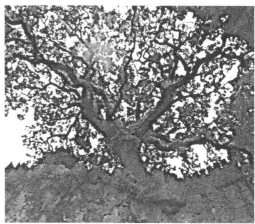

The entire area was reminiscent of a fairytale from the distant past and immaculately maintained with ancient trees and blooming flowers, which made for a spectacular view from every vantage point.

Unusual features surrounded the main building, such as rock towers, symbolic sculptures, ceremonial areas, gardens, grottos, waterfalls, and the much anticipated, Initiation Well. I felt like I had entered a magical place that had very powerful energy, which was both light and dark. I believe that was the overall intention behind the design.

The estate was originally named *Quinta da Torre* in the 1600s and has been renovated several times throughout the centuries until the name was changed to *Quinta da Regaleira* in the 1800s.

The visionary and wealthy owner behind the exquisite property was a man named, Caravalho Monteiro, who bought it in 1892 and hired a variety of artists and architects to carry out his detailed plans. The chief architect was Luigi Manini, who understood Monteiro's vision and devoted himself to designing and creating the estate for several years. After Monteiro's death in 1946, it was sold and had a few different owners until 1997, when it was bought by the Municipality of Sintra and opened to the public.

The features were designed to contemplate many important concepts, virtues, and vices, which have been a part of the human experience since the dawn of civilization. As I walked the grounds, I spotted many symbols and structures associated with Freemasonry, which is an organization fostering esoteric teachings contained in sacred texts. It was founded in England in the 1700s and has since spread throughout the world. There has been speculation, although no connection has been established, that Montiero was a Freemason and that he conducted Masonic initiation rites throughout the property.

There were various rooms, a chapel, unusual locked doors, a Renaissance-style hallway, and Templar crosses inside the main building. It seems that Monteiro had interests in addition to Freemasonry such as the Knights Templar, the Rosicrucians, and the principles of *alchemy*. The alchemical motto *"V.I.T.R.I.O.L."* is an acronym that was written on one of the interior walls; *"Visita Interiora Terrae Rectificando Invenies Ocultum Lapidem (VeramMedicinam)"* which translates to "Visit the Interior of the Earth, and Rectifying (Purifying), you will find the Hidden Stone (True Medicine).[53]

The motto expresses the process of internal, spiritual purification known as alchemy and has been considered the true meaning of *The Philosopher's Stone* in the legend of King Arthur. The tale describes a sacred stone, which was said to hold immense powers of alchemical transformation. It has been veiled in secrecy throughout history, and it was believed that whoever possessed it would gain tremendous wealth, power, and wisdom.

There are two different interpretations of alchemy, one is scientific, and the other is spiritual. The scientific concept is that with certain conditions and combinations of elements, base metals can be transmuted into solid gold. It was believed that only chosen gifted people possessed the ability to complete this process and thusly, became wealthy and powerful. The spiritual idea of alchemy is the belief that the soul has a vibration and frequency, just like light, sound, and matter. During the process of mental and spiritual transmutation through the heart, one can move from a place of lower vibration, self-absorbed ego to a higher vibration of love, compassion, and bliss.

The transformation process consists of working with the *prima materia* (consciousness) and has been called "The Magnum Opus" (the great work). There are seven stages of spiritual alchemy that one passes through on the path to liberating the soul from the confines of the human condition. They are known as, Calcination (humility), Dissolution (letting go), Separation (filtering), Conjunction (re-integration), Fermentation (challenging oneself) Distillation (purification), Coagulation (self-realization). The alchemical symbols have been referred to as the "Language of the birds," which was another synchronistic sign when I made the connection.

I believe that alchemy includes the concept of the Socratic axiom, "Know Thyself," and begins by fearlessly facing old wounds, self-destructive beliefs, and the darkest parts of oneself. The process is complete when the chains of negativity and fear are broken through a variety of methods that promote spiritual purification, a loving state of being, and in effect, a higher vibration.

There is a wonderful book titled *Pearls of Consciousness,* by Christa Faye Burka in which she states, "The heart is like the Alchemist's furnace, it is the place where the gold of the soul is forged."[54]

We entered an area known as *The Threshold of the Gods,* and my attention was drawn to a white marble statue of Hermès Trismegistus, the messenger god, holding his caduceus staff with two entertained serpents, the symbol for both Kundalini and alchemy. I reflected on his teachings in the Kybalion and thought about the simple yet vastly complex wisdom contained in the book, and I was grateful that I was led to discover it.

We walked through an area with two decorative pillars on each side of a Masonic symbol, which was opposite a large throne made of stone with a long slab table in front of it. I didn't know its' purpose, but it felt like a ceremonial space as I sat on the throne and thought about King Arthur's mysterious legend.

I mentally prepared myself and then made my way to the Well, which was located high up on the estate and hidden inside what was made to look like a natural rock formation. I walked towards the round spiral staircase that had nine descending floors, with the bottom one made of marble. The levels represented the nine circles of hell in Dante's Inferno, and the well symbolized the allegory of birth, death, and rebirth.[55]

Carl Jung was very intrigued by the concepts of alchemy, the shadow self, and rebirth. He felt that it was a valuable way to understand and transcend the human psyche. His following quote expresses the polarity principle of transformation, "No tree, it is said, can grow to heaven unless its roots reach down to hell"[56] - Carl Gustav Jung

Before making my descent, I took a photo leaning backward over the top of the well, which marked the beginning of my journey. I walked slowly down the staircase with the walls lined with damp moss and the sounds of dripping water all around. I stopped for a bit and gazed at the marble floor below with the embedded symbol of an eight-pointed star, which represents the concept of resurrection in many ancient traditions, and I felt a strong pull towards it. With each step I took, I wondered about the people who had walked them before me during initiation rites, as well as the thousands of tourists each year.

As I was intuitively performing my introspective initiation, I became aware that alchemy is an ongoing process, as there will always be more obstacles to overcome, more lessons to learn, and more opportunities to transform. I believe that the Philosophers Stone represents the wisdom to know that, be at peace with it, and proceed through life with the realization that all is as it should be.

There was a quote from Beowulf that also came to mind, which I have embraced since learning of it in high school, "Fate will unwind as it must," implying acceptance of the mysteries of life and death.[57]

When I reached the bottom level, I stood in the center of the marble floor and gazed up at the sky above me. There were several dark, damp caves all around, which reminded me of Joseph Campbell's quote "The cave you fear to enter holds the treasure you seek."[58]

I began wandering in the blackness with many hidden gates, entrances, passageways, and dead ends laid out like a maze. As I navigated the caverns, I thought about the metaphor of finding my way through the negative experiences and challenges in my life like a lotus seed finds its way through the mud to blossom into a beautiful flower. The acquired wisdom (treasure) is represented by the lotus, which is why it is such a prevalent symbol of enlightenment.

As I turned a corner, I spotted a light streaming through an opening in the distance and walked towards it to discover a beautiful, glowing waterfall oasis. It represented new beginnings, and I thought of the fact that energy can never be created nor destroyed, it simply changes form. I left the darkness of the well and stepped into the *Garden of Earthly Delights,* which was a stunning display of lush green trees, plants, colorful flowers, grottos, moss-covered waterways, waterfalls, rock formations, and statuary.

As I was emerging from the well, there was a glowing light behind me, and a mysterious man in a long coat appeared in my photo, who wasn't there when I turned around. I walked on stepping stones that were a bit slippery, and I wondered how deep the bright green mossy water was below me as I took each precarious step towards the pathway in the distance. While we were exiting the estate, I noticed a giant tree that was arching to one side, like it was making a statement of total independence by growing in a different direction than the other trees.

I thought about the ideas and emotions I had just explored and felt a powerful sense of balance, strength, inner peace, and excitement about the possibilities that lie ahead. I was ready to embrace whatever changes may come with the acceptance that all is meant to be as it will be. Courage, passion, and a willingness to learn leads to growth.

We hailed a cab to go back to the hotel, and as I got inside, I looked down and saw a cell phone with money and credit cards clipped to it. The cab driver didn't speak English, and as I was trying to explain that I had just found the phone, it rang. The person on the other end only spoke Russian, so I called out around me, "Does anyone speak Russian?" A man responded right away who spoke both English and Russian, and I quickly explained the situation and then handed him the phone, so that he could talk to the man. They planned to meet at the taxi area so he could retrieve it and I felt great making that happen for a total stranger as I got into the cab and we drove back to the hotel.

We arrived at the *Chateau Saudade* and checked into our rooms. As I entered mine, I noticed a painting of a tree with a single bird on the wall, a painted headboard of two trees with a flight of both white and black birds in the center, and pillows with hummingbirds appliqued on them. I was spellbound by all of the symbolism, especially the polarity of the white and black birds, which was the perfect synchronistic message for me after my profound experience. I needed some time to process everything, as I was feeling like something was changing inside of me again. I was glad that we were heading to a resort on the beach where we planned to relax for the next three days.

We went to bed early that evening and woke up with the sunrise to the sound of birds singing outside our window, which opened to a lush, beautiful yard. We packed our things and got ready to meet our driver to head down the coast to the Algarve beach resort area.

We decided to have breakfast at the hotel's *Chateau Saudade Cafe* before leaving the captivating town, and my sister Kim spotted some ceramic birds on the wall that were for sale, so we bought them as a memento of our trip. I wished I was able to spend more time in Sintra, but unfortunately, we were on a tight schedule and had to leave the mystical town, which left a lasting impression on my soul.

Serenity in the Algarve

We arrived at our resort in the early afternoon, checked into our rooms, had a fantastic buffet lunch, and spent the next three days relaxing by the ocean most of the time.

There was a great band playing classic rock at the bar at sunset one evening, and I drank a few too many Espresso Martinis. I most definitely paid for my thrills when I woke up with a headache the next morning, and we had a boating excursion planned for the afternoon. I "toughed it out," and we took a cab to the quaint resort town by the dock. I decided to try the remedy of drinking a bloody Mary to help with the hangover from the night before and actually felt much better after that. It's true what they say about having "a hair of the dog that bit you" after a night of excessive drinking.

As we were walking along the pier, I noticed a man walking past with a tattoo on his leg of the Mayan *Law of Time* symbol, and I thought about the fact that we were there during the Portal Days. I felt that I was being reminded to pay attention.

We boarded the boat, and as we cruised along the shore, we spotted a man fishing off the edge of one cliff and a wedding chapel at the end of another cliff with a marriage ceremony taking place, which was a magnificent place for a wedding. We were in awe of the rock formations and caverns while sailing in and out of the sculptural coves where people were hanging out and enjoying the private beaches.

Our captain ventured far out into the ocean, and we sailed alongside a pod of dolphins enjoying life as they danced in and out of the water. I imagined the feeling of being a dolphin as I watched them gliding through the waves with incredible enthusiasm and joy.

Dolphins can communicate with one another over vast distances through sonar and are highly evolved beings. As a totem, they represent freedom, happiness, compassion, and the release of negative or stagnant energy. They are a reminder to move through life with a playful mindset and embrace the idea of living the moment.

After the fabulous boat ride, we headed back to the hotel and had dinner overlooking the ocean during the sunset on our last night there.

The following morning, we met our driver and drove up the coast to a resort I booked for two days and one night called *The Pine Cliffs*, which was one of the most beautiful places I have ever stayed in all of my travels. It was breathtaking with an assortment of manicured trees, flowers, and red rock formations lining the sweeping coastline, which looked like Sedona on the ocean.

We sat down for brunch and discovered that the resort was also a cat sanctuary, which was interesting considering my recent connection to the cat totem.

We walked from the resort to the beach with the picturesque dunes and rocky cliffs lining the walkway. It was pristine, not overcrowded, and lounge chairs with shade were easily accessible with drinks and food close by in the concession area. We were able to relax and enjoy ourselves without much fuss and preparation beforehand, as everything we needed was right there. I stood on the shoreline, looking out on the vast ocean, and felt grateful to be in such a spectacular place with my wonderful family.

We each got massages in the fabulous *Serenity Spa* and then relaxed in our beautiful rooms with open patios and drank some wine. We truly made the most of the thirty-six hours we spent there.

Historical Evora and The Chapel of Bones

The following day we were scheduled for an eight-hour tour of multiple historic and sacred places, which happened to be on Friday the 13th. We planned to meet our driver at 4:00 AM to drive us to Lisbon so we could leave our luggage at the hotel for the day. While we waited in the lobby, the hotel provided coffee, fruit, and croissants on a cart for us. We thanked them as we said goodbye once our driver arrived.

We got to Lisbon earlier than anticipated and stopped in a cafe for coffee by the hotel before meeting our tour guide. I noticed a flight of black birds on the wall with flower pots dispersed among them and had the feeling that it was going to be a very thought-provoking day.

Our guide met us at 9:00 AM, and we headed out on the road for our excursion. He drove us to our first destination while sharing his knowledge of the history of Portugal and the amazing things we were about to see. We visited a historical town called Evora, which is the capital of Portugal's south-central Alentejo region. It was surrounded by an impressive rock wall, which was built as a fortress in the 15th century by King Afonso IV. Our first stop was an ancient Roman temple built in the first century A.D. in honor of the Roman ruler named Augustus and then later dedicated to Diana, the Roman Goddess of the moon, the hunt, and chastity. It was situated adjacent to the Cathedral of Evora, which was a massive 12th-century Gothic structure with magnificent architectural features.

While we were inside the cathedral, our guide informed us about one of the reasons why Friday the 13th is considered an unlucky day in history. Apparently, on Friday, Oct. 13th, 1307, King Phillip IV of France ordered over six hundred Knights Templar to be arrested, tortured, and executed to suppress their beliefs and gain control of their wealth. I am always fascinated by the varied origins of superstitions.

The entire area had a diverse historical record spanning thousands of years, and our guide kept us captivated with stories throughout the tour. We learned about the Neolithic period to the modern-day and were impressed with the excellent preservation of the monuments that we were visiting. After a great brunch, we strolled along Rua 5 de Outubro, where many shops were selling various handicrafts made from cork, for which Portugal is known, ceramics, and other assorted items. I purchased a Tree of Life dream catcher as another symbolic souvenir from my trip in addition to the ceramic bird from Sintra.

The scenery around the central square of *Praça do Giraldo* was lined with 16th-century Gothic architecture. It seemed so peaceful, but its' history was replete with stories of dark times, as it was the main court during the Spanish Inquisition and was also the scene of numerous protests, rebellions, and violence in the past. We stopped for coffee in a cafe called *Cafe Arcada*, where many famous writers, artists, and musicians have gathered for comradery and inspiration over the years, and I thought again about the book inside of me.

After an inspirational conversation about some famous Portuguese writers and their books while sitting in the cafe, we walked along the cobblestone streets to our next destination called the Chapel of Bones. The town of Evora had over forty cemeteries in the area by the 16th century that were taking up the valuable land, so the Franciscan monks decided to relocate the bones so as not to disturb and condemn the people buried there. They built a chapel to display the bones instead of interring them out of view. They felt it was best to exhibit them to inspire reflection on the transience of the material world and the inevitable transition from life to death. There is a powerful phrase above the chapel door that reads: "*Nós ossos que aqui estamos, pelos vossos esperamos,*" which translates to, "We bones, are here, waiting for yours."

I felt uncomfortable with the message at first and thought it sounded ominous. However, that changed once I spent time among some 5,000 bones and skulls, which were quite artistically displayed on the walls and pillars throughout the small chapel.

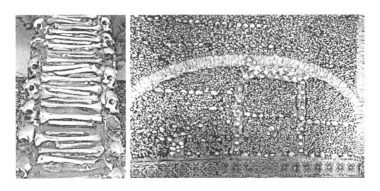

Although the concept and design of the chapel seemed macabre, it evoked a feeling of gratitude within me for the opportunity to live as a human being on the earth. That was the intended purpose of the chapel made clear by a poem written by Father Antonio da Ascencao; "Look, you hasty walker? Stop, don't go furthermore;
No business is more important than this one at your display.
Bear in mind how many were here. Think you'll have a similar end!
Then to reflect, this is reason enough as we all did think it over.
Think, that you fortunately among all the world affairs you do think so little about death. Though if you raise your eyes here stop...as in such a business the sorter you go further, the more get ahead."

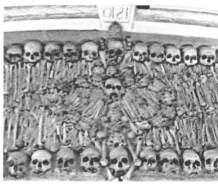

After reading the poem, I reflected on my own life and the Buddhist principles of impermanence and detachment. The chapel began to resonate with me on a deeply spiritual level as I truly grasped the meaning and intention behind the bones – acceptance, faith, fearlessness, gratitude, love, grace, and release of the ego...

I decided to make a video of the interior with my phone when a fascinating synchronistic moment occurred. The crowd was sparse, possibly due to superstition about it being Friday the 13th, so there were only a few people inside. As I scanned from right to left ending the video clip on the entrance/exit, a young girl about six years old with a bright yellow bow in her hair was happily skipping into the chapel, blissfully unaware, right at that exact moment... The juxtaposition of life and death as she entered was intensified by an image on the wall behind her. It was an abstract line drawing of two different versions of parents with an infant illustrating the polarity of human existence, both happiness and despair.

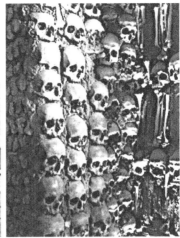

It was a lot to take in as I read the last, ego smashing words;
"The scraggy skulls are my company. I have them night and day. In my memory; Many were honoured in the world by their talents, and other vain ornaments which served vanity. Maybe in Eternity the reason of their torments!"

I recalled the following quote from the Disney Film, *Tuck Everlasting,* which is about a family who drinks from a magic spring at the base of a tree which causes them to become immortal;
"Do not fear death but rather the unlived life. You don't have to live forever, you just have to live"[59]- Natalie Babbitt

I do not feel that death is the end of the road; it leads us to another path in a new direction. We are all on the great cosmic wheel together.

"We bones, are here, waiting for yours."

Dolmens, a Dog, and a Circle of Stones

I was deep in thought as we left the chapel and were driving through the countryside towards our next destination. We traveled on an unpaved road, passing several cork farms along the way to the ancient Neolithic site of the *Dolmen of Zambujeiro*, which was built around 3,000 BC. Our guide informed us that it was the largest of the stone dolmens in Portugal and that scholars speculate that it was once a cemetery and occult center due to the presence of buried human and animal remains in the area. It was very mysterious, and I sensed that it might have been used for both white and black magic rituals. It seemed like a ceremonial space with the giant vertical oblong rocks placed in an overlapping circle and horizontal ones providing a roof structure. Unfortunately, the entrance was boarded up with wood, so we were unable to enter the interior.

It was not a popular tourist spot because it is off the beaten path, and there are only a few people who use the dolmen for rituals on certain days throughout the year. When I thought about the fact that it was Friday the 13th, I wondered why we were the only people there. While we were peering into the cave-like space inside the stones, my sister Laura saw a giant black scorpion, so we decided that it was a sign that it was time to move on from there.

As we were driving to the next site on a winding country road, we spotted a dog on the side of the street that looked as if it was having trouble walking. Our guide pulled over and got out of the van but told us to wait inside in case it was dangerous. When he assessed that the poor elderly dog was thirsty and harmless, he gave him some water, put him in the van, and we brought him to the closest town to try and find his owner. For some reason, we all felt the impulse to turn right once we entered the village and came upon a house with an older gentleman standing out front. When our guide asked him about the dog, he threw his arms up in the air and said something in Portuguese, indicating that it was his dog and that he had been searching for him. We were overjoyed at the happy reunion, as we were all extreme animal lovers with a fondness for dogs. I felt elated when we got back on the road and headed towards the last destination of the tour.

We arrived at Almendres Cromlech, which was another ancient monument located on the slopes of the Monte dos Almendres in Portugal. It is considered to be one of the oldest and most important megalithic stone circles in all of Europe and believed to be about 7,000 years old. Once again, we were the only people visiting at the time, and there weren't any fences or ropes, so we were able to wander freely around the space.

The site consists of ninety standing granite stones arranged in two circles. Scholars have speculated that around 3000 B.C., many of them were repositioned to align with the sun, moon, and stars and that it might have functioned as an astronomical observatory. The stones may have represented gods or deities and had religious significance due to the shape of some of them and the carved symbolic engravings.

The area is still regarded as spiritually potent and sometimes used for rituals and ceremonies. I wondered how many people had been there over the past 7,000 years and how much it had changed due to weathering and erosion since then.

I noticed a beautiful bouquet of purple flowers from the area placed on one of the stones, which looked like a blessing/offering. There were purple butterflies that matched the flowers flying all around me as I laid my hands on the boulders and absorbed the ancient energy. They held incredible stories from the past within them, and I pondered the intention of the people who constructed the site.

I posed for a Natarajasana photo by one of the stones and felt both grounded and free as a bird...

We left Almendres Cromlech after a while and headed back toward Lisbon. We were grateful that we had such an informative guide as he gave us one last history lesson while driving back to the hotel, which was about the meaning of the word *Saudade*. It is an untranslatable Portuguese word that does not have an adequate English equivalent. Loosely translated, it represents a longing or desire for someone or something that was lost and will likely never return.

The concept reminded me of the following quote:
"If you love something set it free
If it comes back, it's yours,
If it doesn't, it never was..."[60] - Richard Bach

The idea of Saudade is a melancholy sort of nostalgia and considered to be a romantic notion of sweet pain. There is a style of Portuguese music called *Fado* (fate) in which the performer sings songs about stories of Saudade, usually with the accompaniment of a guitar or viola. It dates back to the early 1800s and has since been performed in pubs and cafes throughout Portugal. The songs have a somber quality, and the messages are meant to evoke a feeling of "paradise lost." Our guide played some beautiful Fado music for us from his SUV stereo before dropping us off at our hotel. It was quite captivating, and if we weren't so exhausted with an early flight the following morning, we would've considered going to a lounge to see a Fado performance on our last night in Lisbon.

When we arrived at our hotel, we said goodbye to our guide and thanked him for such a memorable experience. It was early in the evening, so we decided to take a taxi to a vegan restaurant for dinner that we found on a website called *www.happycow.com*, which is an excellent resource for vegan and vegetarian restaurants around the world. Our driver only spoke Portuguese and French, which presented a challenge, but I was able to communicate a bit with what I recalled from school and trips to France.

I was reminded of a class I took in college in which we read the book, *Le Petit Prince* (The Little Prince) in French and discussed the meaning behind each chapter. It was written as a children's book for adults by a man named Antoine St. Exupery and is layered with profound symbolism. It's about a pilot whose plane crashes in the middle of the desert. As he is trying to repair it, he is approached by a little prince who takes him on a metaphoric journey through both the positive and negative aspects of humanity represented by people on individual planets throughout the galaxy. He describes the inhabitants of each planet that he visited as either being stuck in a cycle of power and greed or passionate about their causes and responsibilities. It is a great story that helped me to learn some French while exploring some meaningful concepts. One of the quotes that resonated with me from the book was, "It is only with the heart that one can see rightly; what is essential is invisible to the eye." I have always loved that message.[61]

In a strange twist of fate, the author, who was himself a pilot, was flying a plane on a mission during the war in 1944, which mysteriously vanished and was never found. The unusual circumstances of his disappearance, although very tragic and unfortunate, actually enhanced the message of the story.

After conversing a bit with the cab driver, we arrived at the restaurant, which had a sumptuous buffet set up that was some of the best vegan food that I have ever tasted. It was the perfect meal to end our fantastic journey through Portugal, and I was thrilled that we all had such a spectacular time together on our trip.

Birds in Flight

We left Portugal the following morning with incredible memories, and I couldn't wait to return home to begin working on a slideshow of the combined pictures that we all shared. I said goodbye to my family after spending two more days with them as they dropped me off at the airport for my trip home.

I was walking towards the gate and was suddenly compelled to stop in the bookstore. As I entered, it felt as though I was being led to the exact book I was supposed to read, which just happened to be *The Little Prince*... I was instantly struck by the synchronicity that I had thought of the story the night before. I purchased it and couldn't wait to read it on the flight, feeling like there was going to be a message for me.

I recalled that the last time I read it was over twenty years ago to my ex's daughter as the memories of my life with them came flooding back to me all at once. I thought about how change and loss are an integral part of growth, no matter how difficult and painful the process may be.

After reflecting on the past for a while, I boarded the plane and was heading to my seat when I noticed that my ex just happened to be on the same flight... I was stunned but calm as I spoke with him briefly and then took my seat with a feeling once again like I was in a vortex.

In a state of bewilderment, I opened *The Little Prince*, thinking that there would be a sign, and I began reading. I felt so many intense emotions as I turned each page and then got to the chapter where the narrator states, "I believe that for his escape, he took advantage of a flock of wild birds..."

Figure 26

The impact of the moment overwhelmed me as I thought about the synchronicity that seems to occur on airplanes in my life. I had the realization that both birds and planes fly, birds often organize themselves into a synchronized formation, alchemy is referred to as the "Language of the birds," and flying represents freedom... I spent the remainder of the flight trying to piece the puzzle together while contemplating the mysterious ways of the universe. I concluded that I was being divinely guided to decipher the meaning of the signs for myself and bring them together to reveal a pattern. It felt magical.

The Slide Show Lesson
After yet another mind-blowing experience, I arrived home and began working on my slideshow right away while the entire trip was still fresh in my mind. I set up all the pictures and chose songs from diverse bands as background music. I played it through and found that many of the lyrics and photos were synched together perfectly. It would be an almost impossible feat to match them, but it happened several times as if it had been planned.

Unfortunately, I needed to add one more picture that I had on my cellphone and accidentally uploaded all of the photos into my slideshow, which caused my laptop to crash. I was frantically trying to save my pictures and slideshow but to no avail. I called the technical department for help, but there was nothing they could do and suggested that I bring it to their store. I was totally distraught when I thought about all the work that I had just done and the way it lined up so perfectly with the photos and music. I would not have been able to re-create it the same way, and I was also concerned about losing all of my photos and files.

I rushed to the computer repair shop first thing the following morning. As I sat waiting for assistance, I noticed an illustration on the wall of an abstract figure in front of a computer with red birds crashing from above, a child with a rainbow skirt, and a figure with its arms twisted in a spiral. The synchronistic message struck me right away that the red birds symbolized my laptop crashing, and the other two figures were a sign that everything was going to be fine no matter what the outcome. I was informed by a technician that I would have to leave it overnight, and I felt like my Mac was in the hospital as I exited the store while praying for its' recovery.

I began consoling myself with the idea that all of the memories from my pictures had been permanently etched on my mind, and I was ready to deal with losing the photos if my laptop could not be repaired. I also had to accept that many of my videos and other files may have also vanished.

It can be very difficult to feel like there is nothing you can do while you wait for the outcome of an unpleasant situation, but that is a reality that we all face at various times in our lives. I realized that detachment is an incredibly empowering way to handle challenges. Buddha was most definitely on to something.

I went back early the next morning feeling positive as the technician walked towards me with my laptop in his hands and a big smile on his face because he was able to recover everything. I felt relieved as I left the store and very grateful that everything was restored. After that powerful lesson in letting go, I went home and finished my slideshow.

The following day I happened to see a story on TV about a charity organization that helps people with special needs. They were creating painted lighthouses as part of a project to foster inclusion and awareness in the community.

I thought of the special needs students that I have taught over the years and how they have touched my heart with their innocence and adorable personalities. They have been creative, enthusiastic, and capable of producing wonderful, expressive artwork, regardless of their limitations.

I am thankful for the organizations that help people, animals, and the environment and hope to begin a charity someday. I have often envisioned owning a large piece of property where a variety of animals that have been rescued could live and be cared for by like-minded people. It would also include animal therapy for children and adults struggling with anxiety and depression. Perhaps that will become a reality in the future.

The last image from the story was a lighthouse with the phrase, "Be the Light" painted on top, an eight-pointed star on the front, and a flight of birds in the sky...

"Travel Light, Live light, Spread the light, Be the Light"[62] - Yogi Bhajan

Chapter 16
Sequoias & Sunsets

Sequoia National Forest

Portugal rocked my world, and I was glad that I had a few weeks to process everything before my next journey. Nick and I planned a week-long trip to California in July, starting with Sequoia National Park and then heading down the coast to Pismo Beach, Santa Barbara, and finally, a friend's place in Ontario.

On the day of our departure, we decided to stay at a hotel in a town close by the park for the evening so we could wake up early to beat the traffic into the forest. The following morning we entered the park and drove along a winding road for several miles to where the giant Sequoias were gathered. We stopped for a moment to soak in the scenery, and I noticed a store called *Totem Market and Gifts*. I took a picture because I felt that I would begin writing soon and that totems would figure quite prominently throughout my stories.

As we drove closer to the main area of the park, the giant trees were standing like sentinels along the side of the road, and we felt exhilarated while breathing in the fresh mountain air. We arrived at the location in the forest where there was a group of Sequoias named after army generals. They were like ancient ancestors holding the wisdom of nature in their branches and enormous trunks.

General Sherman

As I stood in front of one of the most towering trees in the world named General Sherman, which is believed to be over 2,000 years old, I felt the powerful energy of its presence, and I was humbled.

I reflected on my connection to trees throughout my life, recalling a special tree in my yard that I used to sit under and often climb when I was a young child. I thought of the Gabriel tree in Brazil, the trees in Portugal, and so many other incredible ones that I have encountered throughout my life. Trees are extraordinary and symbolize beauty, growth, perseverance, and the life force within each of us. They are also the lifeline of the planet, contributing to the survival of many species. They represent eternal wisdom in mythologies around the world, such as the Tree of Life, and I believe that they can teach us many things if we quietly observe and listen.

After spending the morning at the park, we drove a few hours down the coast to the town of Pismo and discovered an expansive beach where people were riding horses, camping with and without RVs, and cruising around on quads and other off-road toys. We decided to set up camp and got provisions such as sandwiches, potato chips, beer, whiskey, ice, water, and fire building materials, as we were allowed to have a bonfire until 10:00 PM.

We stayed there all day long while watching the action on the beach, including the birds flying and landing all around us, as we listened to both the sounds of the ocean and hypnotic mood music.

With the brilliant sun setting on the horizon, I did my usual *Natarajasana* pose while Nick built a bonfire in the sand. We enjoyed the rest of the evening together until the fire went out and it was time to head back to town. We had dinner at a fun little bar on the beach and toasted to another great day.

The following morning, we drove to the next destination on our journey, Santa Barbara, and checked into our hotel overlooking the ocean. We relaxed on the beach while watching the boats sail by on the horizon, and I thought about the last time I was there during my yoga teacher training . I remembered feeling anxious about the future, as my life was moving quickly in another direction, but ready to embrace the changes. I realized that I had learned a great deal over the past ten years and also felt very proud of what I had accomplished. It was another full-circle moment on my introspective journey.

As we were leaving Santa Barbara after a couple of days, I asked Nick to pull the truck over because I felt drawn to a store that I saw along the way. He parked, and we entered the shop, which had Buddha statues, spiritual jewelry, tarot cards, and books displayed beautifully throughout the space. Nick suddenly handed me a book and said, "I believe this is what you were looking for." I was instantly struck by the title, *Writing for Bliss* by Diana Raab, and the image of a feather on the cover.[63]

I read the brief description on the back, which was about how to write a memoir, and recognized the undeniable sign that the book inside of me was howling to get out. I bought it, and it turned out to be an insightful and inspiring read, as well as synchronistic in many ways.

Figure 27

Good Omens and the Willow Tree

We arrived in Ontario to where my friend Gina was living at the time. As we were sitting in her yard and catching up with one another, I started telling her about my synchronistic experiences in Portugal when suddenly, a large owl flew directly over our heads out of nowhere... A few minutes later, a scarab beetle flew right onto my hand, as if I needed any more signs of confirmation. Gina took a photo of it as I told her about the synchronistic beetle in Carl Jung's therapy session and that I had planned to write about it in my book. I recalled the time that a beetle appeared on the ground after I had just been reading about the symbolism of the Egyptian scarab. I had taken a photo of it and realized that it looked like it had a pyramid shape on its back that was shining a light into space. We both wondered what the signs meant and discussed the phenomenon that synchronicity often occurs in a pattern of connected messages.

The following day we went to her friend's house, where there was a young man who was an artist with unique paintings that he created in his workshop in the backyard. There was a sign hanging on the wall behind the patio that had birds flying over a sunset that read, *Good Omens,* and I happened to be wearing my flight of birds t-shirt.

Gina showed me his work, and I was drawn to an abstract painting of a Willow tree, which was very meaningful to me. I wasn't sure what it symbolized in the picture, but I felt something very potent hidden in the composition. As she held it up for me to look at it, a beetle was flying in front of the bottom of it, back and forth, like it was sending us some kind of message just like the one who landed on me the previous day...

I was also intrigued by another painting of the trunk of a giant Sequoia tree with two planets next to it and wanted to buy them both. When the artist came over to us, I asked him how much he wanted for the paintings. He responded that the Willow tree was a terrible painting and that he planned to either throw it out or paint over it. When I told him that I loved it and would be happy to pay him for it, he adamantly refused to sell it to me and walked away. I knew that I needed to hear about the symbolism because I had a feeling that it was important. I went inside the house to where he was playing pool and started talking to him about synchronicity. I explained that I was drawn to it immediately and that a beetle was flying in front of it that seemed to be attempting to communicate a message to us when suddenly, he

213

looked like he had seen a ghost. He said that he painted the composition soon after his uncle's passing and that the beetle represented his uncle for a personal reason that he didn't want to disclose. He then proceeded to point out a hidden image of an owl that he painted in the tree, knowing nothing about the significance for me... Gina and I were surprised because neither of us noticed the owl in the painting at first. I briefly explained the synchronicity of the owl and that the tree reminded me of a Willow tree growing in my yard with my dogs' ashes placed in a living urn in the soil beneath it. He looked stunned once again when he informed us that his uncle was symbolically buried in an urn under the tree in the painting... I sensed a shift in his energy as he went from guarded and defensive to deeply moved and peaceful. After a moment of contemplation, he said, "Take both paintings, they're yours" and wouldn't accept any money for them. I thanked him profusely and told him that his act of generosity would bring him *Good Omens*.

Upon returning home, I spent the rest of my summer break on my patio in deep thought. I went back to work at the beginning of the school year with a constant feeling that I needed to write but was only able to compose a couple of sentences at first. I had a tremendous amount of material, which was overwhelming, and I didn't know where to begin. I started creating an outline but then discarded it soon after feeling that the words needed to flow freely. I decided to put it on hold until I was ready. I believed that I would be given a sign, and then it would just happen. Well, happen it did.

"There is no greater agony than bearing an untold story inside you."[64] - Maya Angelou

Part Six

Wisdom & the Wolf

The Wisdom of the Owl

The Instinct of the Wolf

Chapter 17
Athena and Anubis

The French Quarter - NOLA

My friend Danielle from college invited Nick and me to celebrate her fiftieth birthday in New Orleans the weekend before Halloween. I was excited to be a part of her celebration and had a feeling that the trip would provide some inspiration for my writing. I designed a costume to represent Athena, the Greek goddess of wisdom who was considered a strategic warrior of words and initially depicted as an owl before the Greeks gave human forms to their pantheon of gods. In essence, Athena and the owl are one and the same being, and according to myth, an owl sat on Athena's blind side to enable her to see the truth.

Danielle also invited another couple that she and her husband Steve are friends with, and we all got along well. We had a great spot on the balcony of a bar called *The Cat's Meow* one evening, which Steve arranged so that we could throw Mardi Gras beads to the crowd below. I thought about the symbolism of the cat totem and wondered if it may be a sign for me considering the name of the club. Danielle was about to toss some beads when I noticed a large emblem hanging at the bottom with the number fifty on it. I pointed out the synchronicity, and she decided to keep them.

After having a fabulous time on the balcony, we decided to walk around the French Quarter to check out some shops and music venues. I spotted a statue of Ganesha in a storefront window, and I made a mental note of his presence as a sign to be *vigilant and aware.*

We happened to find a store with a car out front that had a mosaic design with a Grateful Dead theme covering the exterior. We went inside the shop, which was filled with very unusual things, and I noticed a sign that said *Live a Great Story*, which most definitely resonated with me, as well as some Grateful Dead artwork. I ended up buying a bracelet cuff that has a cutout of a hummingbird at the top, and the words *Free Spirit* etched into the metal, which turned out to be quite synchronistic later on.

The following day we decided to take a boat trip on the Bayou and had lunch that afternoon at a local cafe. Danielle received the number fifty to set on our table for the server to bring the food to us. It was so cool that the number, which was a sign for both of us, appeared twice in such unusual ways.

After the cafe, we decided to go our separate ways and then meet up in the French Quarter later that evening, as it was our last night in New Orleans. Nick wasn't feeling well, so I agreed to meet them on my own while he stayed back at the hotel to recuperate. I joined my friends, and we decided to go to a famous Absinthe bar where we met a couple who were dressed up as Mulder and Scully from the X files for Halloween. They suggested that Danielle and I drink the *Butterfly Absinthe*, which we did, and toasted to turning fifty and our friendship of over thirty years.

The butterfly symbolism of transformation inspired the realization that we had both entered another stage of our lives, and it made me think about the way the aging process is perceived differently by people, depending on their values and experiences. Cultures around the world describe the changing stages of life through childhood, adolescence, adulthood, and old age as rites of passage with each period being special and unique. I have always felt that age is not something to be feared and fought, and I was glad to be at a point in my life where I embraced the idea that "with age comes, wisdom."

My friends decided to turn in early, and I wanted to check out the music scene, so I decided to go out on my own. Before they left, Steve gave me ten extra drink tickets for *The Cat's Meow* in case I decided to go back there so I could give them away. I was staying about four blocks from Bourbon Street, so I felt pretty comfortable in my surroundings. As I finished my Butterfly Absinthe, the words "Enjoy life like a rock star" came to mind, so I ventured out to the French Quarter to be a part of the vibrant energy, as a woman walked by me in a butterfly costume...

There was a band playing in the first bar I entered that was taking requests, so I asked to hear some Led Zeppelin. I waited to see what song they would choose to play while thinking of the lyrics to a particular song, and it was the one they played next... I left there soon after and went back to *The Cat's Meow*. While I was up on the balcony again, there was a group of young men hanging out looking like they were having a lot of fun. I started speaking with one of them who informed me that it was his bachelor party with nine of his best friends, so I gave them the ten drink tickets, and they were very appreciative.

After hanging out at the bachelor party for a bit, I wandered in and out of various music venues and ended up in a country-western bar. I noticed that there were images of the round plastic pieces that went in the center of old forty-five record albums back in the day being reflected on the dance floor. It made me think about how much music has meant to me throughout my life and what a huge Stevie Nicks fan I was in high school when a woman suddenly walked up to me and said, "Has anyone ever told you that you have a Stevie Nicks vibe?" I thanked her for the compliment, while also appreciating the synchronicity, and decided it was time to end the evening on a high note and head back to the hotel. I don't have a great sense of direction and forgot which streets to take, so I checked my phone navigation map because I was on a side street with no one around to ask directions. It wasn't giving me the correct information, and I didn't want to take the chance of getting lost and possibly ending up in a dangerous situation, so I began thinking of other options such as walking back to the main area. I recalled seeing Ganesha in the storefront a few days prior and decided to call upon him. Luckily, at that moment, a woman whom I noticed earlier from my hotel appeared and I asked if I could walk back there with her after explaining that I was unsure of the correct streets to take. She happily obliged, and I got back to my room, safe and sound. As I was drifting off to sleep, I thought about how things tend to fall into place for me when I focus my attention on a positive outcome. I have been involved in many dicey situations in life, which could've had a different result each time. I believe that through intuition, we can recognize the possibility of danger and attract a protective field of energy around us like a cloak to thwart negativity. I could have decided to walk back to the hotel by myself, gotten lost, and ended up involved in a dangerous ordeal, being that it was late at night in New Orleans. I was glad that the woman from my hotel just happened to be walking past at that moment and also thankful for Ganesha having my back once again.

I have learned to trust my instincts and intuition, which has served me well, but I do not take either for granted. Sometimes the choices that we make don't have the desired outcome, and we must learn from the experience. If we trust in the process, it seems that the benevolent forces in the universe guide us in a way that illuminates the path.

Anubis, the Egyptian Cat, and the Wolf
The following morning Nick and I decided to get breakfast across the street from where my friends were staying. I left the house without my gemstone bracelet, which had an Anubis charm on it, and I felt compelled to go back inside to get it for some reason. We entered a food court style café, and I saw a sign for Egyptian food, which I love, so I headed in that direction. I approached the counter and noticed a statue of Anubis with a white Egyptian cat sitting to the left of it. Incredibly, the Anubis statue was identical to one that I own, and it sits on the same side next to a black Egyptian cat in my home...

My head was reeling as I waited for my meal to be prepared, and I thought about how Anubis had made a few appearances as of late. I also noticed that my journey totem, the wolf, had been showing up in unusual ways as well. I recalled the fun I had by myself the night before, and a metaphor of the wolf in my life, as I enjoy being a part of a wolf pack, but also enjoy being a lone wolf. A few minutes later, a man walked by wearing a shirt with an image of a wolf's head on the front that said *Lone Wolf* underneath it... He was with a group of people, so I didn't want to bother him with a strange request of asking if I could take a picture of his shirt. As I was leaving the cafe and about to walk out the door, I noticed an owl on the back of a woman's shirt and took a photo. The fact that Anubis, the owl, and the wolf appeared together, along with the cat totem, had me wondering what was next.

We arrived at the airport in the early afternoon, and I stopped at the bar to have a mimosa before the flight. I sat next to a woman wearing a T-shirt, and I could see a tiny bit of her tattoo peeking out from under her sleeve. Considering what had transpired that morning and that I often have synchronicity happen on planes, I asked her if it was an owl tattoo. She lifted her sleeve, and indeed, it was, so I asked her if I could take a photo for the book I was about to write, to which she agreed.

To top it off, we all boarded the plane, and our friends were seated in the row right in front of us, even though we booked the tickets several weeks apart without discussing any information prior to purchasing them. I reminded Danielle of the synchronicity that occurred when we first met in college, with my phone number written on her Grateful Dead cassette tape. Although she is not usually interested spiritual subjects, she agreed that the universe works in mysterious ways.

The Cat and the Dog

When I returned home from New Orleans, I felt that something was brewing in connection with the totems, and I wondered if maybe I was supposed to get a cat. I started looking at some photos of cats that were up for adoption and saw a Savanah cat with a gorgeous brindle coat, so I did some further research about the breed. After reading about them, I realized that it wouldn't be a good fit for me, and decided to wait and see if a cat just happens to cross my path someday.

I thought about the fact that my statue of Anubis was identical to the one in the cafe, so I decided to do some research about him in connection with the wolf. I had always thought he was a jackal and was amazed to discover that he had been misinterpreted throughout history and that he was actually considered to be an ancient Egyptian wolf... The pieces of the puzzle seemed to be coming together, and I wondered where the signs would lead me. I got my answer later that week when I decided to go shopping at a local store and drove past a pet supply supermarket that was having an adoption event.

I felt compelled to park and go inside because I wanted to be around animals and saw that there were about seven black cats up for adoption as I entered the store. I thought that it was a sign that I was meant to adopt a black cat and asked the volunteer if I could hold one of them. Although she was adorable, something didn't click energetically, and I handed her back to the woman while explaining that I was a dog person. I was about to leave the store when she remarked that there were two adorable puppies that I should check out around the corner. I told her that I was not interested in getting a dog, as I had recently lost my beloved Pomeranian named Sable, who lived by my side for twenty years.

Towards the end of Sable's life, she taught me a great deal about dying gracefully. As I observed her in the final weeks of her decline, she was unsteady and incoherent, but I felt her wanting to hang on a bit longer for some reason.

I often insulate myself against feeling pain and discomfort by suppressing my emotions as a self-preservation reaction to an otherwise gut-wrenching, heart-shattering feeling. I tried to make her as comfortable as possible, fed her, and kept an eye on her when I could, while I put my heart in a closed box so as not to feel the pain. On the day of her transition, she was slowly slipping away as I held her in my arms all morning in my yoga room, and I played a beautiful Aum chant as I felt her spirit ready itself to let go.

Nick and I brought her to the vet to make the transition peacefully and painlessly. As we approached the door, the wind picked up suddenly, and she lifted her head to feel it upon her face one last time. She loved the wind so much during her life that she would often sit outside my bedroom door on the balcony basking in the sun on a breezy day.

As she took her last breath, I felt her beautiful spirit leave its' vessel as the tears began streaming down my face. I was so grateful that Nick was there to comfort me as I was so distraught, but at the same time relieved, that she was free from her suffering.

My other dog, Amber, passed away several years before Sable. She was equally special to me and also loved to sit in the sunshine on breezy days. Their ashes have been growing within a Willow tree in my yard, which is why the painting I mentioned earlier was so special to me. I placed an angel statue by its' trunk to watch over them, and I can feel their essence whenever the wind blows.

Amber   Sable

As I turned to walk out of the store, the volunteer said once again that I should just look at the puppies. I finally caved and walked over to the adoption area. As I looked down into the pen, an adorable brindle mixed breed munchkin looked up at me with his puppy dog eyes, and my heart melted. I asked the volunteer if I could hold him, and then once I had him in my arms, I couldn't put him back down. I spoke to the woman in charge of the adoption process and asked if she had any information about him. She told me that he was from a litter of thirteen, and his mother's name was Sativa, which was a sign for me, so I decided to take him home and named him Marley after Bob Marley.

I was totally unprepared, so I purchased a crate, food, toys, a leash, and a collar. It was a snap decision, especially because I was resistant to getting another dog, but I believe that fate brought us together. I thought about the way in which the cat totem, through both the black cats and the brindle Savannah cat, actually led me to Marley.

When he was home in his crate and sleeping on his back, I noticed that he had three significant markings on his body. The one on his belly looked like a wolf's head, the white patch on his chin was in the shape of a crescent moon, and the white fur on his chest looked like a hummingbird, which was part of the bracelet that I bought in New Orleans. I happened to be wearing it, along with my Anubis bracelet, that afternoon.

I reflected on the synchronicity in the breakfast cafe and realized that I was given signs that I would find Marley. I feel that he has come into my life through Anubis to teach me some valuable karmic lessons. He has been instinctually trying to be the alpha wolf, and I have learned to put my love for him aside and assert myself as the leader of the pack. He even reminds me of a wolf when he does a slow, wolf-like walk and howls when he plays with his squeaky toy.

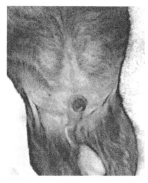

I discovered through a DNA test that Marley is a mixture of four different breeds; Rottweiler, Boxer, Terrier, and Newfoundland. I could never have imagined that I would adopt a male mixed breed dog that would grow very large, as I have only ever had small female dogs. It was a significant change for me, and I am so glad that I took on the challenge because I know that he will grow up to be an incredible companion. I have accepted that he will test me with his puppy antics until he is a bit older, which has been a valuable experience in learning to be more patient. He is affectionate, loving, and playful, and when he looks through me with his soulful eyes, I know in my heart that he is worth all the effort.

We take long walks every day at both sunrise and sunset, often stopping by my favorite inseparable horses to give them carrots. I love him unconditionally and am so glad that the volunteer at the pet shop was relentless in suggesting I check out the puppies before I left the store. He has enhanced my life tremendously, and I look forward to spending time with him every day.

Marley has been a catalyst for my writing from the beginning of my book to the final chapter. It would have been written quite differently if he hadn't entered my life. His presence has also inspired me to explore the concepts that I have written about more in-depth, such as patience, compassion, selflessness, acceptance, detachment, and persistence. The *Trust your Instincts* wolf poster that I mentioned in an earlier chapter just happens to be hanging on the wall next to a Bob Marley picture in my home. It was all meant to be.

The Wolf Blood Moon Eclipse

"There is a battle of two wolves inside us. One is evil. It is anger, jealousy, greed, resentment, lies, inferiority, and ego. The other is good. It is joy, peace, love, hope, humility, kindness... The wolf who wins is the one we feed."

I decided to create a gemstone necklace to symbolize my connection to the wolf and owl totems. I ordered a wolf pendant carved from a gemstone called labradorite, as well as a string of faceted labradorite beads from two different overseas companies, and they happened to arrive at the same time in the mail. Labradorite is a stone with properties of helping to increase one's psychic awareness and intuition. I envisioned using moonstone, hematite, and pyrite gemstones in the design as well. Hematite is a grounding stone associated with the Root Chakra representing stability, strength, and survival. Pyrite is associated with the Sacral and Solar Plexus Chakras representing abundance, creativity, and manifestation. Moonstone strengthens the heart and crown chakras. The combination would resonate with the balance between the lower and upper chakras. I also planned to incorporate a special owl bead.

While I was contemplating the necklace, I happened to be watching a show on television about the Vikings when suddenly, a wolf appeared on the screen followed by an owl seconds later... Another fascinating thing about the episode was that one of the Viking characters had just begun embracing Buddhist teachings after a chance meeting with a monk. I was astounded by the synchronicity of seeing both the wolf and the owl, as well as having written about my connection to Buddhism and the Vikings. I decided to make the necklace a few days later because there was going to be a lunar eclipse coinciding with the full *Wolf Blood Moon* that evening. It turned out just as I had pictured in my mind's eye.

As the sun began setting, I invited my neighbors over to view the eclipse, and Nick built a bonfire in our backyard. We were eagerly awaiting the transition but were concerned that we wouldn't be able to see anything due to the thick cloud cover. The fire was roaring as we focused our energy on the sky clearing. Much to our amazement, the clouds began dissipating, and the eclipse became visible from the initial stage through to completion. Marley was with us, as we all began howling at the luminous moon in the starry night sky above us.

It occurred to me that during an eclipse, from any vantage point on the earth, the moon seems to be the same size as the sun, yet it is significantly smaller. For them to appear to have the same circumference, they would have to be situated in the exact location that they are, relative to each other and the earth, which could not possibly be a random coincidence.

I went to sleep that night, after thinking about how synchronicity has so positively affected my life. The events have been indelibly imprinted on my soul and now they are shared through my stories and pictures.

As I continue to navigate the voyage that lies before me, I am grateful for what has been and excited for what will be.

To be continued...

Epilogue

"You will either step forward into growth or step back into safety"-
Abraham Maslow

As I have cycled back through my life experiences, I have realized that my quest is a continuous voyage, both outward and inward, with a circular destination. Writing my memoir has been an incredible, cathartic, ride down memory lane that has enabled me to re-live the moments which so profoundly affected me.

I believe that each person's journey is linked to their karma. We all experience both the darkness and the light throughout our lives in varying degrees. How we perceive and react to circumstances, sentient beings, and our environment determines our karmic path. Free will allows us the opportunity to manifest our desires and reach our highest potential. The challenges or successes that happen along the way are unique for each person's transformation and growth.

I have always been fascinated by the idea of self-actualization being a heightened state of awareness and bliss based on self-reflection and gratitude. The concept was first developed by Abraham Maslow, an American psychologist, who proposed that healthy human beings have a certain number of needs that are arranged in a hierarchy, with some needs being more primitive or basic than others. He wrote a paper in 1943 called "The Theory of Human Motivation," in which he comprised a five-tier model of human needs, often depicted as hierarchical levels within a pyramid. From the bottom of the pyramid upwards, they are; physiological, safety, love, belonging, esteem, and self-actualization.[65]

Self-actualization is at the apex of the pyramid and is the full realization of ones' potential through the fulfillment of dreams and desires. It usually occurs later in one's life through many varied experiences and epiphanies that have culminated in wisdom, happiness, and inner peace. People who have reached this stage often feel that they have fulfilled a higher purpose in their lives. They are unaffected by other people's opinions, are typically non-judgmental, and their presence is both comforting and inspiring.

"Follow your bliss and the universe will open doors for you where there were only walls"[66] - Joseph Campbell

I have "followed my bliss" and learned valuable lessons along the way. I have been fortunate to have traveled to many countries and bear witness to the ingenuity, superb artistry, craftsmanship, and imagination of the human race. Although self-actualization is at the apex of Maslow's pyramid, it is the trek up the steps of the pyramid, not arriving at the peak that matters most. My experience of hiking up Huayna Picchu in Peru is a metaphoric example of this idea as I felt exhilarated by the challenging effort that brought me to the top of the mountain. I reaped the reward of my climb towards my destination by the feelings evoked by my journey. "Life is a journey, not a destination."[67]

Self-actualization is a state of being that enables one to feel balanced and at peace on a deep soul level. It is the realization of being connected to every aspect of the entire universe and that we are one same consciousness. Science teaches us the concept that nothing is separate on the atomic level; therefore, separateness is an illusion. Many cultures have understood this wisdom since the dawn of civilization. It is known as *Maya*, which is a Sanskrit word for illusion. The Mayan civilization wholly embraced the concept of Maya, hence the name, and the Mayan idiom *In Lak'ech* means "I am you, and you are me." The Native American phrase *Aho Mitakuye Oyasin* means "All my relations-we are one."

The past, present, and future are also not separate. Life is a voyage to be navigated with an awareness that everything happens in the moment of now. We are co-creating our existence, second by second, while living within it. The past and the future can only exist in the present, as it is only in the moment that I can reflect on my life or ponder the future.

Humankind is at a crossroads in the ability to sustain our species, along with many others, on our planet. We must awaken to the realization that what we do, think, and say has a ripple effect on one another, all aspects of our environment, and consciousness as a whole. At this point, we will have to unite to repair the damage of our continuous mistakes and wastefulness. The future of the human race is in a race against time, and we must embrace the aspects of compassion, gratitude, love, unity, and balance for our survival. Animals are being abused and slaughtered for human consumption, greed, and blood-thirsty entertainment. Our environment is being destroyed at an alarming rate due to many factors such as the meat and dairy industry, plastics, carbon emissions, fracking, and the list goes on... Rather than be a part of the problem, we can choose to be a part of the solution in a way that utilizes our talents, abilities, and passions. I believe that each person can make a difference in ways that can collectively bring about change on a larger scale.

Trees are our lifeline, and yet the forests are being decimated all over the world by the ridiculously profitable multinational companies, as well as many smaller industries choosing profit over life and the environment. I wrote a poem about deforestation many years ago from the perspective of a tree.

The Tree
I live in the soil as a tiny seed
Sunshine and water is all I need
I emerge slowly from the dark
As my body forms a protective bark
My branches reach towards the light
While a weary traveler rests from flight
I have many needful friends close by
From the deepest forest to the open sky
Who depend on me to make a home
So they no longer have to roam
My life allows others to exist
As I try my hardest to persist
Until the axe cuts through and shatters my core
So I can't provide shelter anymore
With my parts divided and shipped away
My weeping soul is left to decay
But somewhere in the wounded soil
A seed lies waiting amidst the turmoil
Trying with all of its' powerful might
To reach out to the nurturing sunlight
There needs to be a master plan
To stop the destructive force of man - Susan Heather Ross

This Lakota prayer expresses my immeasurable gratitude for the life I have been given on this miraculous planet.

"To the creator for the ultimate gift of life, I thank you.
To the mineral nation that has built and maintained my bones and all foundations of life experience, I thank you.
To the plant nation that sustains my organs and body and gives me healing herbs for sickness, I thank you.
To the animal nation that feeds me from your own flesh and offers your loyal companionship in this walk of life, I thank you.
To the human nation that shares my path as a soul upon the sacred wheel of Earthly life, I thank you.
To the Spirit nation that guides me invisibly through the ups and downs of life and for carrying the torch of light through the Ages, I thank you.
To the Four Winds of Change and Growth, I thank you.
You are all my relations, my relatives, without whom I would not live.
We are in the circle of life together, co-existing, co-dependent, co-creating our destiny.
One, not more important than the other.
One nation evolving from the other and yet, each dependent upon the one above and the one below. All of us a part of the Great Mystery.
Thank you for this Life."

Soon after writing the prayer above, I came across this amazing art installation of the word **Love,** with hundreds of tiny birds cut out of the metal throughout the letters.

Just wow...

Notes

[1] Jung, C.G, *Psychological Types, or, The Psychology of Individuation* (Harcourt, Brace, 1923) Conclusion, p. 628

[2] Redfeld, James, *The Celestine Prophecy,* (Warner Books, Inc. November, 1997)

[3] Jung, C.G, *Synchronicity: An Acausal Connecting Principle,* (New Jersey Princeton University Press, Princeton, 1969), p. 22

[4] Jung, C.G., *The Archetypes and The Collective Unconscious Collected Works of C.G. Jung Vol.9 Part 1* (Princeton University Press, 1981)

[5] Jung, *Synchronicity*, p. 21

[6] Einstein, Albert, *A Letter Addressed to Max Born,1926*

[7] Campbell, Joseph, *Reflections on the Art of Living: A Joseph Campbell Companion,* Joseph Campbell Foundation, edited by Robert Walter, conceived by Diane K. Osbon (Harper Collins, New York, New York, 1991), p. 8,18

[8] Moyers, Bill D, *Power of Myth Interview Series*, (Public Broadcasting Service, June 21, 1988) Documentary, Miniseries

[9] Campbell, Joseph, *The Hero with A Thousand Faces*, (New World Library, 2008) 3rd edition, Joseph Campbell Foundation

[10] Campbell, Joseph, *Reflections on the Art of Living: A Joseph Campbell Companion*

[11] Campbell, *The Hero with A Thousand Faces*

[12] Moyers, Bill D, *Power of Myth Interview Series*

[13] Bach, Richard, *Illusions: The Adventures of a Reluctant Messiah*, (Dell, October 10, 1989)

[14] Barefoot Sanctuary, www.wolfkin.ca / jada@barefootsanctuary.com

[15] Pinkola Estes, Clarissa, *Women who Run with the Wolves: Myths and Stories of the Wild Woman Archetype,* (Ballantine Books,1992)

[16] Crystal Magic, 2978 W.SR. 89-A, Sedona, Arizona 86336

[17] Jada Fire and Stacey James, *Ancient Animal Wisdom*, (U.S. Games Systems Inc.; Box Tcr Cr edition, July 9, 2014)

[18] Enchantment Resort, 525 Boynton Canyon Road, Sedona, AZ 86336

[19] Jung, Carl and Anelia Jaffe, *Memories, Dreams and Reflections*, (Pantheon Books, 1963)

[20] Capra, Bernt, Byars, Floyd & Capra, Fritjof, *Mindwalk*, producer- Klaus Lintschinger, director-Bernt Capra (Triton Pictures, Sept.9th 1990)

[21] Chopra, Deepak, *Spontaneous Fulfillment of Desire*, (Harmony; Reprint edition, August 12, 2004)

[22] The Grateful Dead, *Fire on the Mountain*, Album - Shakedown Street (Arista Records, 1978)

[23] Nicks, Stevie, *Wild Heart*, Album - The Wild Heart, (Producer: Jimmy Iovine, Gordon Perry, Tom Petty Label: Modern / Recorded: Autumn 1982 – Spring 1983 Released: June 10, 1983)

[24] Lennon, John, The Beetles, *Lucy in the Sky with Diamonds*, Album - Sgt. Pepper's Lonely Hearts Club Band (George Matin, EMI Studios, London, 1967)

[25] The Grateful Dead, *Scarlet Begonias*, Album - From the Mars Hotel (© Universal Music Publishing Group, Warner Chappell Music, Inc,1974)

[26] The Grateful Dead, *Truckin'*, Album - American Beauty (Warner Bros., 1970)

[27] Hans, Jenny, *Cymatics: A Study of Wave Phenomena and Vibration*, (Macromedia Publishing; 3rd edition, July 1, 2001)

[28] Burka, Christa Faye, *Pearls of Consciousness*, (Brotherhood of Light, Inc., Albuquerque, New Mexico, 1987) p.31

[29] Mandelbrot, Benoit, *The Fractal Geometry of Nature*, (Times Books; 2nd prt. edition, 1982)

[30] Mandelbrot, Benoit, *The Fractalist: Memoir of a Scientific Maverick*, (Pantheon Books, October 30th 2012)

[31] Jung, Carl Gustav, *"Memories, dreams, reflections"*, (Random House Inc. 1973)

[32] Fulghum, Robert, *All I Really Need to Know I Learned in Kindergarten,* (Ballantine Books, May 4th 2004)

[33] Einstein, Albert, (attributed to him but not substantiated)

[34] Blavatsky, H.P., *The Secret Doctrine, the Synthesis of Science, Religion and Philosophy - Vol 1. Cosmogenesis, Vol 2. Anthropogenesis* (Theosophical Publishing Company, 1888)

[35] The Three Initiates, *The Kabbalion,* (White Crane Publishing; Revised, Updated edition, February 8, 2011)

[36] Lederman, Leon, *The God Particle: If The Universe is the Answer, What is the Question?* (Mariner Books; Reprint edition June 26, 2006)

[37] Decarte, Renee, *The Treatise of Man,*1637, *The Passions of the Soul,* 1649

[38] Khalsa, Harbhajan Singh, *3HO, Sikh Dharma International,* founded in 1969

[39] Van Gogh, *Letter to brother, Theo van Gogh,* 1888

[40] Pantajali, *The Yoga Sutras,* 400 CE

[41] Von Goethe, Joanne Wolfgang (August, 1749 - March, 1832)

[42] Greger, Michael with Stone, Gene, *How Not to Die,* (Flatiron Books, 175 Fifth Ave. New York, NY, 10010)

[43] Hendrix, Jimi, The Jimi Hendrix Experience, *Are you Experienced?,* Album - Are you Experienced? (Track Records, 1967)

[44] Silverstein, Shel, *The Giving Tree,* (Harper and Row, Oct. 7th, 1964)

[45] Hamilton, Bethany, *Soul Surfer: A True Story of Faith, Family and Fighting to Get Back on the Board, (MTV Books, June 6th, 2006) Movie: Soul Surfer,* (Director: Sean McNamara, 2011)

[46] Proust, Marcel, *Remembrance of Lost Time,* (Modern Library; 2012)
[47] Proust, Marcel, *Remembrance of Lost Time*

[48] Osorio, Cristina, *Synchronistic Voyage,* book cover designer, www.Samsarascenes.com (info@samsarascenes.com)

[49] Tolkein, J.R.R., *Lord of The Rings,* (George Allen and Unwin, July 1954)

[50] Arguelles/Valum Votan, Jose, Foundation for the Law of Time, https://lawoftime.org

[51] Chopra, Deepak, *Synchrodestiny*, (Ebury Pr; New Ed edition May 31, 2005)

[52] Rowling, J.K., *The Harry Potter Series*, (Bloomsbury Publishing, June 1997- July 2007)

[53] L'Azoth des Philosophes, 15th century Alchemist, Basilius

[54] Burka, Christa Faye, *Pearls of Consciousness*, p. 16

[55] Alighieri, Dante, *The Divine Comedy (Dante's Inferno)*, 14th century

[56] Carl Gustav Jung, Aion:Researches into the Phenomenology of the Self, The Collected Works of C.G. Jung, (Princeton University Press, Part 2 / Volume 9, June 17th 1979)

[57] Unknown Author, Beowulf, c. 700–1000 AD (date of story), c. 975–1010 AD (date of manuscript), (Thorkelin, 1815)

[58] Campbell, *The Hero with A Thousand Faces*

[59] Babbitt, Natale, *Tuck Everlasting,* (Disney, 2002)

[60] Bach, Richard, (attributed to him but not substantiated)

[61] St. Exupery, Antoine, *Le Petit Prince (The Little Prince),* (Mariner Books: 1st edition, May 15, 2000)

[62] Singh, Harbhajan (Yogi Bhajan) August 26, 1929-Oct. 6th 2006

[63] Raab, Diana, *Writing for Bliss,* (Loving Healing Press, September 1, 2017)

[64] Angelou, Maya, *I Know Why the Caged Bird Sings,* (Ballantine Books; Reissue edition, April 21, 2009)

[65] Maslow, Abraham, *A Theory of Human Motivation,* (published in 1943)

[66] Campbell, Joseph, *Reflections on the Art of Living: A Joseph Campbell Companion*

[67] Emerson, Ralph Waldo (attributed, but not substantiated)

List of Figures

Front Cover - Cristina Osario - www.Samsarascenes.com

Figure 1 - Totem Animal Painting
Image: Painted by Olivia Taylor (one of my wonderful yoga students)

Figures 2 and 3 - Animal Spirits Book
Image: Author Nicholas J. Saunders - Time Life Books(Inc.), (Duncan Baird Publishers,1995)

Figure 4 - Mirror Owl Reflection Picture
Image: Jada Tam (www.wolfkin.ca)

Figure 5 - Bad Owl Cafe
Image: Bad Owl Cafe, Las Vegas, NV

Figure 6 - Sand Mandala
Image: Goldstein Gallery, Sedona Arizona

Figure 7 - Student Mandala
Image: J. Jamjulee S.

Figure 8 - Blue Medicine Buddha
Image: Painted by Sherab Khandro (Shey)
Goldstein Gallery, Sedona Arizona, www.GoldsteinArt.com

Figure 9 - Skull Asteroid
Image: Photo by NAIC-Arecibo/NSF
Image: Artist rendering by Jose Antonio Penas/Sinc

Figures 10, 11 and 12 - The Hansom House, Southampton NY
Image Credit: Raymond Palma, raymond_palma@ymail.com

Figure 13 - Cymatics Wave Resonator
Image Credit: Richard Morrow, www. rmcybernetics.com

Figure 14 - Flower of Life and Sri Yantra
Image: Flower of Life in Abydos, Egypt
Image Credit: Sri Yantra - Wikipedia Commons - Author Ranjithsiji Source - own work

Figure 15 - Leonardo da Vinci's Mona Lisa and Last Supper
Image Credit: Mona Lisa / Last Supper - www.Sacred_Geometry.com

Figure 16 - Leonardo da Vinci's Vitruvian Man and Moon/Earth
Images Credit: Andrew Hoskins - www.elementalorgone.co.uk

Figure 17 - Leonardo da Vinci's Vitruvian Man with Fibonacci
Image: Andrew Hoskins - www.elementalorgone.co.uk

Figure 18 - Cardioid Graph Image
Image: Precalculus - Graphing, Numerical, Algebraic - Addison Weseley Longman Inc.

Figure 19 - Cardioid Equation
Image Credit: Cardioid Equation - Wikipedia Commons - Benutzer: Ag2gaeh
Source - own work

Figure 20 - Kundalini
Image Credit: Wikipedia Commons - Author - Silvanasono
Source - own work

Figure 21 - Spider Image
Image Credit: Wikipedia Commons - Author - Arnaldo de Souza Vasconcellos
Júnior   Source - own work

Figure 22 - Spider Image
Image Credit: Downer, Steve, www.wildlife-cinematography.co.uk

Figure 23- Angel Gabriel Card
Image: *Angel Therapy Oracle Deck* by Doreen Virtue, Ph.D

Figure 24 - Intender's Handbook
Image: Tony Burroughs - published by New Leaf Distributing Company; 1st edition (May 1, 1999)

Figure 25 - Integrity & Intention Poster
Image: Artist - Devin Mulanax

Figure 26- The Little Prince
Image: St. Exupery, Antoine, *Le Petit Prince,* (Mariner Books: 1st edition, May 15, 2000)

Figure 27 - Writing for Bliss
Image: Raab, Diana, *Writing for Bliss,* (Loving Healing Press, September 1, 2017)

Index

Denmark, 39, 40, 41

Desa Seni, 31, 160,

Detachment, 27, 31, 32, 38, 96, 181, 199, 207, 225

Dolmens, 43, 201

   Stonehenge, 43, 44

   Zambujeiro, 201

   Almendres Cromlech, 202-203

Dominical, Costa Rica, 143, 145

dream catcher, 131, 197

Druids, 44

The Dali Lama, 31

DMT, 102, 127

DNA, 123, 124, 173, 225

Durga, 156

E

Eastern Philosophy, 56,

Egg of Life, 79

Egyptology, ix, 15, 40

Eiffel Tower, 56

Eight Limbs, The 122

Emerald Tablets, 15, 56

Estey Pump Organ, 176

Evora, 195, 196, 198

Eye of Horus, 123

F

Fado, 204

Feather of Truth, 15

Fibonacci Sequence, 82, 83

Flower of Life, The, 77, 78, 79, 80, 81, 96, 236

Fruit of Life, The, 79

Foundation of Law of Time, The, 173, 174, 235

Four Realms, (Kabbala) 97

Freemasons, 184, 185

Friday the 13th, 195, 196, 199, 201

G

Gabriel, 18, 19, 21, 22, 23, 136, 137, 154, 210, 237

Ganesha, 129, 135, 136, 155, 156, 162, 168, 169, 182, 217, 219, 220

Garuda, 161

Gautama, Siddhartha, 32,

Gayatri Mantra, 167

Genesis Pattern, 78